A Guide to the Gospel Parallels

Mark, Matthew, and Luke:
A Guide to the
Gospel Parallels

A Companion for Individuals and Study Groups
to the *Gospel Parallels*
of Burton H. Throckmorton, Jr.

Neal M. Flanagan, O.S.M.

The Liturgical Press

Collegeville   Minnesota

ISBN: 0-8146-1005-6

DEDICATION

To my family—
in gratitude

Table of Contents

Introduction

Origin and Purpose
of the Book

For a number of years now I have given to students for the ministry a course on the Gospels of Mark, Matthew and Luke—the three *Synoptic* (can be seen together) Gospels—using Burton H. Throckmorton's *Gospel Parallels* as the basic text. I have also given numerous brief lectures and workshops on these same gospels to groups of non-specialist lay people interested in the Bible. With these latter groups it was impossible to spend the time necessary for a discovery of the riches that evolve from a comparative study of the gospels, though it was abundantly clear that the people involved were intensely interested in such a project. Hence this book.

It hopes to be of service in classroom situations where the teacher can use it, adjust it, challenge it, and where the students will have an instrument to use at home as they assimilate the gospel versions to make them relevant to their own lives. Apart from classroom context, it also hopes to be a "Do-it-yourself" or, better, a "Do-it-your-selves" book to enable individuals and groups lacking a professional teacher to study the first three gospels by investigating them as they appear in parallel columns. This comparison, hopefully, will note what the three—or at least two of them—have in common both in content and sequence, as well as how they differ in both. It will also make evident material which is the unique property of only one of the three.

The *Gospel Parallels* gives us a remarkable instrument by which we can—presuming the necessary time and industry—get inside of an evangelist's head so as to know his individual style, purpose, audience, and theological emphases. This *Companion,* there-fore, hopes to be an aid to teacher and students in a classroom situation, as well as to individuals and groups interested in the study of the gospels but lacking a trained teacher. In broad terms it will first make a comparative study of the three gospels. When this is completed, it will attempt a summary treatment of the individual evangelists, of Mark's Gospel, of Matthew's, of Luke's. This type of summary should be done, it appears to me, only after the work of comparison has been finished.

A Guide to the Gospel Parallels

Chapter One

The Gospels: What They Are Not and What They Are

Strange, perhaps, but it is easier to say what a gospel is *not* than to define precisely what one is. In fact, there is probably no even relatively simple definition of a gospel that is accepted without some adverse criticism by all New Testament scholars. As a literary form, the New Testament gospels are unique in the history of literature. No such simple description as "Lives of Jesus," "Profession of Faith," "Words and Deeds of Jesus," "Christian Ethics," comes really close to explaining precisely what they are.

But let us begin with what they are not, and the main point to emphasize here, because it is so all-important, is that the gospels are not *profane history* books giving us quite simply the life of Jesus of Nazareth, what he did and said and how he died. To call the gospels histories is to place them in a definite literary category, and even a little reflection will show us that they do not fit in that bag.

Profane history centers on facts and their *secular meaning*. History is not simply a collection of facts, a chronicle of events, but also a scholarly attempt to find the secular meaning connected with them. Why did they happen? What was the result? Do the effects remain, and in what way are they still visible? Take, for example, the introduction of Africans into North America as slaves. What were the reasons for, and the consequences of, this traffic in human beings? What did that whole series of inhuman events mean to the enslaved Africans, to their sellers, to the buyers? What effects remain visible on the American scene today? These are the historical questions which search for the secular meaning of those past events.

The gospels are also interested in events, in happenings—the material of history. But the meaning they search for is the God-meaning (theology) of the historic event which was the life of Jesus of Nazareth. What was the God-meaning of his birth, of his works, his death and resurrection? What did and do his statements mean for our salvation? These are questions outside of the historical context. God-meaning is perceived and explained not by historical criticism but in faith explicated by reason and expressed in creed and worship.

History is also vitally interested in *dates and places,* the so-called eyes and ears of history. The historian wants to know, must know, the when and the where, so that he can situate events in time and geography. How different are the gospels! What emphasis, for example, do the first three gospels give to dates? Can you remember off-hand any dates at all which can be found in them? Mark begins with the preaching of John the Baptist. And when was that? You'll not find out from Mark. Matthew initiates his version of the good news with a long chronology of Jesus' forebears which ends with Mary's pregnancy. And when was that? Herod the Great appears in the infancy account and *secular history* can give us dates for him, but Matthew certainly does not. Nor does Luke in his infancy account, though he does introduce Caesar Augustus (Lk 2:1) into the story and he, too, can be dated by historians. Only in Lk 3:1 is there an attempt at dating which is at all reminiscent of the historical manner of writing. The gospels are just not all that interested in exact times.

Their interest in places is almost equally weak. The Synoptists have a simple over-all geographic scheme which, since it also appears in the Acts of the Apostles (10:36-40), may well have served as the basis for the earliest Christian preaching. Jesus moves from his baptism in the *Jordan* close to Jerusalem up north to *Galilee* for his ministry and then down to *Jerusalem* for his death. *Jordan to Galilee to Jerusalem*—that is the basic itinerary. Some events are connected in the earliest Christian tradition to definite places: even more are recounted without a specific location at all. The Synoptists frequently tie incidents together—like beads in a necklace—by the arbitrary use of "And then . . ." or "Next . . ." Exactness in time and place is not a gospel strong point.

Profane or secular history must also be careful about quotations, *careful to produce the exact words used by the speaker.* In the gospels, on the contrary, the substance of the sayings more than suffices. It was a period which lacked dictaphones, shorthand, newspaper reporters and cameras. It was also a period in which the evangelists felt quite free to make significant changes which would enable them to make their own teaching more evident.

Consider, as a few examples among numerous possibilities, the two different versions of the beatitudes found in Mt 5:3-12 and Lk 6:20-23 (cf. *Gospel Parallels* [G.P.] #19); the differing texts of the Our Father in Mt 6:9-15 and Lk 11:2-4 (G.P. #30); the words of Eucharistic institution at the Last Supper (G.P. #236); the inscription on Jesus' cross (G.P. #249); the profession of both Peter at Caesarea Philippi (G.P. #122) and that of the centurion beneath the cross (G.P. #250).

History, finally, must attempt to treat *all relevant facts,* from the beginning and in order. Otherwise there is danger of supposed history turning into propaganda. Now, while it is true that the Synoptic Gospels of Mk, Mt, and Lk are quite similar, yet it is also true that they differ extensively in choice of incidents, in emphasis, in manner of description and in order. They do not simply record incidents in chronological order; they structure them so as to serve their theological purpose.

Take Luke as an example. He has no difficulty in eliminating material found in the other Synoptists. The second multiplication of the loaves (G.P. #118), found in almost identical form in Mk and Mt, disappears in Lk, as does the distasteful story of the death of the Baptist, a story of weaving hips and bloody head which appears in both of the other Synoptists (G.P. #111). Lk can also rearrange order. The calling of the first disciples in Mk and Mt (G.P. #11) is postponed till later in Lk (G.P. #17) even though this means that Simon's mother-in-law is introduced to us in Lk 4:38 (G.P. #13) before we have met Simon himself. And when Lk finally does introduce the first disciples (G.P. #17) he includes within the simple account evident in Mk-Mt (G.P. #11) the attractively apropos story of a miraculous draught of fish which resembles in striking fashion a similar story in the final chapter of John's Gospel (Jn 21:1-14). The evangelists obviously feel free to eliminate material, to reorder it, to make additions. This is not the historical procedure. And that is just the point. Though the gospels deal with historical events, their authors write as theologians, as men who write out of faith and to inspire faith.

Profane history, therefore, is not what the gospels are. Granted! But what in fact are they? That is a difficult question, and any correct answer to it must be complex and nuanced. As I see them, the Gospels are the GOOD NEWS *of* Jesus and *about* him. By that I mean they contain the exciting news proclaimed *by* Jesus that God's reign had arrived, that God's presence within the world and within people of faith was being effected. This meant a call to conversion, to a change of both outlook and living patterns. "The reign of God has arrived! Change!" That was the good news of Jesus, in the sense of the news proclaimed by him.

But the gospels are also, and primarily, the good news *about* Jesus, that is that God's presence—curing, comforting, compelling, challenging—had arrived in Jesus himself and had been made manifest in that special personal integrity which balanced Jesus' word and deed in perfect harmony. The risen Jesus was recognized and proclaimed as Lord, as Son of God, as Christ-Messiah, and this recognition, this profession, became an integral part of the good news, an integral part of what we mean by a written gospel.

This good news about the risen Jesus was first *preached,* preached by the apostles, as well as by those Spirit-filled Christians whom Paul calls prophets, teachers, and preachers (1 Cor 12:28; Rom 10:14-15; 12:6-8). Convinced that they possessed the Spirit (cf. Paul in 1 Cor 7:40), they not only related what Jesus himself had said and done but expanded upon it through applications and examples which they found necessary and profitable for their local Christians. And so the accounts about Jesus were maintained and developed through preaching, through catechizing, and through the liturgy both of baptism and of the breaking of bread. In the Eucharist, especially, were the stories of Jesus told, his words repeated and explained, applied, and developed—a process which the Christians were certain was inspired and controlled by the Spirit (cf. Jn 14:26).

Finally, into the picture come the evangelists, Mk, Mt, Lk, who somewhere between the years 70-90 put into their present form the gospels which bear their names. These men were not mere collectors who gathered the material that came to them into an unorganized lump. It is the studies made in our own twentieth century which have demonstrated in clear fashion that the evangelists were, indeed, true authors, men of creative talent even when working with material common to the Christian churches, men who wrote for different communities, who had different purposes and emphases, and who saw the meaning of Jesus in differing fashions. Each was his own man, with a strong individuality that makes itself evident throughout his writing.

The gospels, therefore, are the literary end-products of a complex and multiple Christian effort which

a) began with Jesus;

b) continued after the resurrection with the study, teaching, and preaching of the apostles, teachers, evangelists, prophets, and preachers;

c) was strongly influenced by use of Jesus-material within Christian worship, especially the Eucharist and baptism;

d) and was finalized by the individual gospel writers, each fashioning the material along the lines of his own and his community's interests and problems.

Chapter Two

A Basic Assumption:
The Two-Source Theory

The Theory

Before passing from the preceding brief consideration of the gospels themselves to the direct work on the *Gospel Parallels* which is the aim of this *Companion,* we will have to pause to examine an assumption upon which much of our work will be based. It is called the "Two-Source Theory" of the Synoptic Gospels and believes—with considerable force of argument and an equally considerable backing of scholars—that both Mt and Lk possessed, while writing their gospels, two main sources.

The first source was the Gospel of Mark, either in the precise form in which it has come down to us or in a form very similar to our own. The second was a collection of Jesus' sayings, commonly called "Q," perhaps from the German word "Quelle," meaning source. Originally composed in Aramaic, Q was quickly translated into Greek. Both Mt and Lk had individual copies of Greek translations. These copies were, at times, identical: at other times, perhaps due to changes which crept in through frequent use, simply similar in substance. Unlike the Gospel of Mark which gave a connected account of Jesus' works and words from the baptism till resurrection morning, Q would have been simply a collection of Jesus' words placed together with little or no attempt at order. Only a very few narratives would have been included in this Q, or *sayings,* material. This is the basic outline of the theory. In graphic form it presents itself:

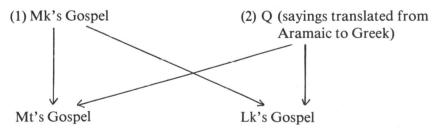

5

This basic two-source theory easily breaks down into an uncomplicated four-source proposal since it becomes immediately evident to any Gospel reader that Mt has material peculiar to himself, which derives from neither Mk, Q, nor Lk and that Lk also has special material not found in the other sources. If we designate Mt's special material as M and Lk's as L we get the following illustration:

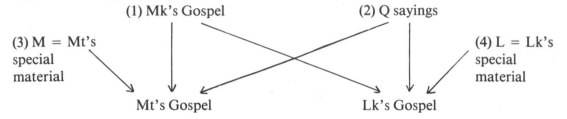

In summation, then, the two-source theory believes that Mt is dependent on Mk and Q, but with added material special to himself: that Lk is dependent on Mk and Q, plus material special to himself. The basic two-source theory, consequently, expands itself easily and without complications into a four-source theory.

Foundations for the Theory

So much for the theory, but what solid foundation supports it? Why not simply say that Mk, Mt and Lk wrote quite independently of each other, and that their striking resemblances rise simply from the fact that they are narrating similar or identical teachings and narratives originating from one and the same individual, Jesus of Nazareth? The difficulty with such an explanation is that it is all too simple and disregards with an almost blatant blindness the striking *literary* similarities and identities which can be found throughout the three texts. It also disregards frequent identities in sequence as evangelists agree in ordering episode after episode of Jesus' life. This will become a living reality for us as we work through the *Gospel Parallels,* but for the moment I would like to give just a few examples of literary similarities which postulate some form of interdependence on the part of the Synoptists.

Let's consider Q material first. Look at G.P. #2 entitled John's Preaching of Repentance. This is sayings material shared by Mt and Lk (Q). Once the introductions are over with—and they differ in both since they were not contained in the original sayings source—the words of Jesus are identical from start to finish except that "fruit that befits repentance" of Mt's verse 8 becomes plural in Lk, and Mt's "presume" in verse 9 is rendered "begin" in Lk. Apart from that, the citations are the same—sixty out of the original sixty-three Greek words are identical. Or try G.P. #34, Words of Jesus on Serving Two Masters. Except that Mt has "No *one*" and Lk "No *servant*" the quotations are the same—twenty-seven of the twenty-eight Greek words found in Lk are exactly the same in Mt.

These are just a few of the multiple *sayings* passages which are shared by Mt and Lk. If you had two students turn in examination papers in which the literary likenesses were so striking, you could hardly help but wonder. Here, too, it seems that either Mt is copying from Lk, or Lk from Mt, or both Mt and Lk from something which they share in common. It is this latter possibility which has, after intense examination and discussion, been adopted by the majority of biblical scholars and which has given rise to the Q postulate. In simple phrasing this means that where Mt and Lk share material in common which is not found in Mk—and this is almost exclusively sayings material—this derives from an original Aramaic collection of Jesus' words which go back to the early pre-Gospel period of the first century. Both Mt and Lk would have had a copy of it in Greek translation.

A second body of material which argues for the interrelatedness of the Synoptists rather than for their independence is the omnipresent abundance of material shared by all three. This is called in scholarly language, triple-tradition material, that is, it is shared by all three evangelists. In passage after passage Mk, Mt and Lk share the same narrative or the same teaching in texts which are virtually the same, differences being frequently explainable on the grounds of grammatical preferences or precision—Mk, for example, loves the present tense which the other two regularly change, and he frequently offers a complicated text which the others tidy up. Examples of the triple-tradition are G.P. #13, The Healing of Peter's Mother-in-Law; G.P. #45, The Healing of a Leper; G.P. #52, The Healing of a Paralytic; G.P. #53, The Call of Levi. The examples are so numerous that these few must suffice for the moment.

In instance after instance the three Synoptists narrate the same episode, in almost the same words, and frequently in the same context or sequence. In these instances, too, some theory of interdependence seems necessary. The weight of scholarly opinion leans heavily in favor of Mk as the connecting link, as the *first* Gospel which was thereafter used by both Mt and Lk in their "revised editions."

Discussion on this point is by no means terminated and other theories have been, and are being, advanced—some extraordinarily complicated. But belief in the priority of Mk and its subsequent use by Mt and Lk still holds the field, and it is this theory which we will be using as we study the *Gospel Parallels*. One of the strongest of the many arguments in its favor is that it works! Presuming the priority of Mk, presuming its use by both Mt and Lk, one can gain a remarkable insight into the theological minds of Mt and Lk by observing how they amend, omit, and rearrange the Markan text, an insight which will echo that which results from a study of Mt and Lk on their own. The theology of Mt and that of Lk which results from a study of their individual gospels is paralleled by that which rises from observation of the types of changes they make in the Gospel of Mk.

Cautions

It would be dishonest and unscholarly to present the two-source theory as a proven fact. It is not. It is still a theory, but the best theory now available. It does not, however, answer all the questions nor explain all the gospel phenomena. There are some instances where Mt and Lk agree in wording against Mk—as though either Mt had Lk or Lk had Mt—and such agreements are not always easily explained. And there are equally baffling instances in which Mt and Lk agree in lacking a Markan passage. Why such an omission if both have Mk and neither has the other? These are real difficulties, and the solutions offered have not always been persuasive. But these phenomena are not strong enough to seriously weaken the solid arguments in favor of Mk's priority and of the use of both Mk and Q by Mt and Lk.

Chapter Three

A Study of the Gospel Parallels Index: The Sequence of the Synoptists

With this chapter we turn our attention directly to the *Gospel Parallels,* specifically to pp. xx-xxvi which give us the Index. What I hope to do is to show how, on the basis of the two-source theory, Mt and Lk ordered their gospels using Mk as their frame, as their skeleton. At times one or the other will leave Mk's order, or change it, but the Index will indicate the points of both departure and return. Often the visual picture offered by the Index is so clear that the observer can see, without difficulty, precisely what Mt or Lk is up to. But this will become evident only as we get into this study.

The first thing to note on p. xx is that there are only two *Infancy Narratives*—Mk has none—and that these two narratives by Mt and Lk are not set out in parallel columns but simply printed one above the other: Mt as "A," Lk as "B." This tells us something in itself. The narratives are not paralleled because they cannot be: they are quite different and independent one of the other. Of the four divisions in Mt — Genealogy, Birth, Magi, Flight and Return—only the Birth of Jesus appears in the Lucan division. Of all the material given in both stories, only a few common elements can be detected: for instance, Joseph and Mary, the Spirit-conception, birth at Bethlehem, and a subsequent residence in Nazareth. Notwithstanding the obvious importance of these elements, the accounts are essentially different. They are of different emphases—Mt's centers on Joseph, Lk's on Mary—of different origins. They are not meant to be harmonized, and actually cannot be.

The most surprising thing about them, it seems to me, is that though neither of these written accounts seems to have influenced the other in the least, yet both Mt and

Lk do have such material as introductory to their gospels. Why this happened, we have no idea. A simple glance, then, at the top half of p. xx tells us that we are working with two—and only two—infancy narratives which are completely independent one from the other.

I. THE GALILEAN SECTION

This brings us to the bottom half of p. xx, The Galilean Section, and with this the parallel columns begin. Perhaps we should pause here for a moment to see how the columns are laid out. The first entry reads:

		Matt	Mark	Luke	Matt	Mark	Luke	Page
1	John the Baptist	**3:1-6**	**1:1-6**	**3:1-6**	11:10	1:15	7:27	8

This tells us that episode (or paragraph, or pericope) #1 concerns John the Baptist. The reference to John is followed by 3 columns (we will refer to them as columns 1, 2, 3), *all in heavy print* which indicate that this first episode is found in the same place, the beginning of Jesus' public ministry, in the triple-tradition, in Mt 3:1-6; Mk 1:1-6; Lk 3:1-6. These three columns of Mt, Mk, and Lk are the most important in the Index and attention should be paid especially to them. They can be found, as we see in the final column on the far right, on p. 8 of the G.P. They are followed by three intervening columns (4, 5, 6) *not in heavy print,* in which reference is made to other material in the three gospels which is either parallel to, or a doublet (repeat) of the material found in columns 1-3. In this instance reference is made in columns 4-6 to Mt 11:10 which is similar to Mk 1:3, to Mk 1:15 which echoes Mk 1:4, and to Lk 7:27 which is the same as Mk 1:2. Columns 4-6 can, at times, give us valuable information, but most of the time we will be talking about columns 1-3, the *heavy print* references to Mt, Mk, and Lk.

Let's attempt to enter our Index study by a simple and brief consideration of episodes #1-17. Even this is enlightening. You can see as you move patiently from this explanation to the consecutive episodes in the Index that #1 is shared by all three evangelists; #2 is common to Mt and Lk; #3 is peculiar to Lk; #4 is shared by all; #5 is Lk's; #6 is in common; #7 is Lk's; #8-9 are common; #10 is Lk's; #11 is shared by Mt and Mk; #12-15 by Mk and Lk; #16 by all three; #17 is Lk's.

A general visual impression is that both Mt and Lk have basically the same sequence as Mk, but that Mt substracts from it while Lk adds. Mt substracts from Mk material concerned with miracles, and this we see in #12-15. But this material will not get lost. It will turn up later in Mt ch. 8, where Mt has begun to gather together a whole group of Jesus' miracles. Later study will indicate *why* Mt does this. Lk, on the contrary, adds material and does a bit of changing around, but his frame of order is still essentially that of Mk. He adds #2-3, the preaching material of the Baptist. He adds #5, John's imprisonment since, for Lk, the Baptist is to step off the stage as Jesus steps on. One important character at a time is enough, especially since the Baptist for Lk is an Old Testament representative, the last of the prophets, one who must vanish as *the* prophet, the New Testament prophet, replaces him. Lk also adds #7, his version of

Jesus' genealogy, different from that of Mt which introduced the latter's infancy narrative.

The most striking changes made by Lk, however, occur in #10, 11, and 17. Paragraph 10 treats of Jesus' rejection by his fellow citizens of Nazareth, an episode recounted much later (cf. columns 4 and 5) in Mt 13 and Mk 6. Lk has thus, and deliberately, managed to give us, right from the beginning of Jesus' ministry, an overall view of what will happen to him: initial success, hostility, violent death. The passage is Luke's overture to the whole Gospel. Paragraph 11 is striking in that Mt and Mk's call of the first disciples is missing at this point in Lk. It will, however—as can be seen in column 6—show up later in Lk 5:1-11, which is #17, The Miraculous Catch of Fish. Perhaps Lk felt that the response of the disciples to Jesus would be better understood if it followed the miracles of #12-14.

Take a final look now at p. xx. The infancy narratives are found only in Mt and Lk, and they cannot be paralleled. Paralleling begins with ch. 3 in both Mt and Lk, which is the equivalent to ch. 1 in Mk since he has no infancy chapters. At this point our eyes tell us that both Mt and Lk have sequences very similar to Mk's, but that Mt at this point subtracts from it while Lk adds. As we get to know Mt and Lk better, it will be possible to make intelligent guesses as to *why* Mt and Lk act here as they do.

This carries us over to p. xxi. Our eyes tell us in vivid fashion what is happening. Mt is doing all kinds of things on his own. He was together with Mk and Lk back at #16, and will be with them at #45 and in the three successive passages from #52-54. So he has not lost track of Mk—nor has Lk—but has moved away for a moment to do his own thing.

And what is that? You can see back at #16 where the three evangelists were all together that Mk, followed by the others, begins to describe a preaching journey in Galilee. He does it in just one verse (Mk 1:39). Mt builds up that one verse into three (Mt 4:23-25) since he wishes to have a more impressive introduction, an introduction to the abundant material you can see outlined on p. xxi, #18-44. This is Mt's Sermon on the Mount, and with this the Index gives us a visual demonstration of one of Mt's most characteristic literary techniques. Five times—this is the first—during the course of his Gospel he moves away from some suitable and preparatory spot in Mk to weave together a sermon-shaped collection of Jesus' sayings regarding some fairly specific theme. This first time it will be Jesus' inaugural address, the spelling out of the main Christ-stance for Jesus' future disciples.

Columns 2 and 3 are empty at this juncture since neither Mk nor Lk is producing anything similar to this sermon at this point. Columns 5 and 6 are interesting, however. Column 5 (Mk) tells us that very little of this sermon material has any echo in Mk. Mk is weak on sayings, and Mt is here strengthening Mk's weakness. But look at column 6, that of Lk. It becomes evident that almost all of Mt's sermon is found in Lk, but not at this point. Which is to say that most of the sayings material which Mt has added to Mk is also in the hands of Lk and will be included in his Gospel, too. But in places different from those selected by Mt. This is what we previously spoke of as the "Q" phenomenon.

May I ask one further task for the moment, but a very simple one? Note how much of this sermon material of #18-44, found in Mt chs. 5-7, can be found (cf. column 6) in Lk 6! This, as we shall see, will be Lk's Sermon on the Plain, similar to this present sermon of Mt's, yet considerably shorter.

Paragraph 44, then, is the conclusion to Mt's Sermon on the Mount, and here we meet a distinctive and important Matthean characteristic. The text of #44 (Mt 7:28) reads, *"And when Jesus finished . . .,"* an English translation of the six Greek words with which Mt concludes all five of the great sermons found in his Gospel. This five-fold occurrence of an identical formula has indicated to numerous scholars the main divisions in Mt's work. Some refer to these five divisions as Mt's five Books or Mt's Pentateuch.

But now back to the Index, this time to look over #45-63. The initial impression given by columns 1-3 is that Mt is again at work building up the material found in Mk and shared also by Lk. Mk's sequence (as also true of Lk's) is #45, The Healing of a Leper; #52, The Healing of the Paralytic; #53, The Call of Levi; #54, The Question about Fasting. Mt uses all of this material and, in the case of #52-54, in the same sequence. But to it he adds #46-51 and #55-63.

What is he doing? Well, he is certainly amassing a large collection of miracle stories, mostly healings. To that of the leper (#45) and the paralytic (#52) already present in Mk he has added those of the centurion's servant (#46), Peter's mother-in-law (#47), the Sick at Evening (#48), the Storm (#50), the Demoniacs (#51), Jairus' Daughter and the Hemorrhaging Woman (#55), the Two Blind Men (#56) and the Dumb Demoniac (#57). Just the abundance of these miracle stories collected into one spot is striking and must be intentional. This intentionality becomes even more evident when we note (cf. column 5) that #47-48 had already appeared earlier in Mk 1:29-34, and that Mt skipped over them at that point so that they could be used here. By checking the same column 5, we can observe that #49-51 are set here in Mt even though he found them later, but in the same sequence, in Mk chs. 4-5. Mt quite definitely wishes to build up his Gospel at this point with *miracle stories* and with references to discipleship (cf. #49 which Mt adds to the discipleship material already contained in Mk, #53-54).

What Mt is doing with these changes is preparing for his next sermon. It is a sermon on discipleship and runs through #58-63. Its immediate introduction is The Sending Out of the Twelve (#58) and it concludes (#63) with Mt's specific formula: "And when Jesus had finished . . ." (Mt 11:1). What we have seen here is Mt again using Mk as a skeleton (#45, 52-54) on which to enflesh his expanded version. And we have seen him insert his second sermon—that on Christian discipleship—for which he prepared by assembling material on miracles and discipleship. Part of this he already found in Mk at this juncture; the rest he added on either from other sections of Mk's narrative or from Q since #46, The Centurion's Servant, is shared by Mt with Lk as is evident from column 6.

This has brought us to the top of xxii where Mt ends his sermon with #63. What happens next, say from #64-89? One simple answer emerges: Mt is on his own from #64-68; material is generally shared by all three in #69-72; Lk is on his own from #73-84; Mt and Mk are mainly together from #85-89. Easy enough, but can anything more specific be said about the use being made of this material by the evangelists?

Mk's sequence is that of #69-72, 85-86, 89, a block of material that first leads to the call of the twelve (#72) and then speaks of Jesus' true relatives as those united to him, not by natural family ties, but through obedience to the will of God (#89). Mt uses every bit of this Markan material except for #72, The Call of the XII, which he has already used at #58 to prepare for the Sermon on Discipleship. But he adds to Mk's paragraphs additional material (#64-68, 87-88) which he believes suitable to prepare for the third sermon which will follow, beginning with #90.

But it is Lk who is visibly doing his own thing at this point. Let's fix our attention on him for just a moment. He has been proceeding step-by-step with Mk, at his side through #45, 52-54, 69-72, eight successive paragraphs, except for inverting Mk's sequence of #71-72. This inversion enables Lk to place the Call of the XII first, then to bring Jesus down from the hills onto the plain where he can meet the sick and diseased, and in their midst preach what must be called in Lk's Gospel (in contrast to Mt's) the Sermon on the Plain. This is Lk, ch. 6 (#73-78). It is considerably shorter than Mt's inaugural Sermon on the Mount, but a glance at column 4 shows us that Lk's material is also to be found in Mt, especially in his chs. 5 and 7 where the Sermon on the Mount is located. What Lk is doing here, consequently, is what Mt has already done, that is, moving away from Mk's sequence for a moment to insert a Jesus-sermon into his Gospel. Before returning back to Mk, Lk adds another interesting block of material, #79-84. It consists of "L" material—only in Lk—concerning women (#80, 83-84), a Q item (#79), and John the Baptist material, also Q, in #81-82. These last two Baptist paragraphs have already been used by Mt back in #64-65.

Our journey now has taken us as far as #90 where we can begin to look at #90-104. We are moving into parable material. Mk offers three "seed" parables, the Sower (#90), the Seed Growing Secretly (#95) and the Mustard Seed (#97), plus explanations and a presentation of the purpose of the parables. Mt does what we might now expect Mt to do. He takes over the Mk material (except for #95, the Seed Growing Secretly) but adds on to it a wealth of other material, forming the whole into Jesus' third sermon, that on the parables. Mt is able to add to the Seed parables those of the Weeds (#96), the Leaven (#98), the Hidden Treasure, and the Pearl (#101), the Net (#102) and the Householder (#103). This is so very typical of Mt's compositional activity.

Lk, as we see from column 3, is going in precisely the opposite direction from Mt. Rather than adding to Mk, he subtracts from him, concentrating exclusively on the parable of the Sower (#90, 93) and the purpose of the parable (#91, 94). And, in a surprising move, he adds to the sower parable paragraph #104, Jesus' True Relatives, which both Mk and Mt had used back at #89. By so doing, Lk has Jesus relate his mother and brothers to those "who hear the word of God and do it." This corresponds to Lk's desire to present the mother of Jesus as a model of the disciple who lives in obedience to the word of God (Lk 1:38; 2:19, 51).

The next section we want to look over is a fairly long one, #105-136. Fortunately, however, it is not difficult to analyse if one will simply move slowly—but confidently —through the material. The most obvious phenomenon is the amazing correspondence in sequence between Mt and Mk. Mt lacks #105-107 because they are miracle stories that he has already used in his collection of the ten miracle stories that form his chs. 8-9 (cf. column 4). But starting from #108 you can see that he is moving right along with Mk through #132. Mt lacks #109 because he has already used it (col. 4); lacks #121, the Blind Man of Bethsaida because he does not follow Mk's theology that the apostles, like the blindman, could not see (believe) until Peter's profession at #122; omits the Strange Exorcist (#130) as irrelevant to his fourth Sermon on the Church which begins at #129; and skips #132 on the Salt which he has already used for the Sermon on the Mount (cf. col. 4). But the rest of the Markan material he has, and in exactly the same sequence as Mk!

Not surprisingly, he has also added material. This we see in #128, The Temple Tax, a story about Peter in whom Mt is especially interested at this part of his Gospel. But the main additions are #133-136 since Mt has used the particularly apropos section of #129, Mk's account of the Dispute about Greatness, to begin the fourth sermon of Jesus, the Sermon on the Church, that is, on the relationship which should exist between the members of Jesus' Church. It might be of value to note at this point that, apart from occasional omissions and additions, Mt follows the sequence of Mk almost exactly from #110-253. This amazing identity in sequence must be one of the most compelling arguments for the literary relationship between the two Gospels!

What is Lk doing at this point? He is with Mk from #105-107. He omits #108, Jesus Rejected at Nazareth, because he has already used it way back at #10, as an overture to the whole Gospel story. He is with Mk from #109-112 except for the gruesome story of John's head on a platter (#111), a banquet dish too strong for Lk's taste. Again Lk is with Mk from #122-130 except for #125, The Coming of Elijah, since Lk much prefers to present Jesus himself—rather than the Baptist—as the New Testament Elijah figure.

With all this striking similarity in sequence between Lk and Mk it is amazing to see one whole block of Markan material disappear in Lk #113-121. This is called Luke's *Great Omission*. It seems that at this point Lk began to realize that his Gospel might be in danger of becoming too lengthy, too unwieldly, and that he omitted this whole Markan section with the justification that much or all of it was similar to material presented elsewhere in Mk. The most obvious similarity in material is #118, The Feeding of the 4,000, which is so similar to #112, The Feeding of the 5,000.

In general, then, it can be seen that #105-136 are a remarkable and visible illustration of identity in sequence between the three evangelists. Mt follows Mk, but adds; Lk follows Mk, but subtracts.

II. LUKE'S SPECIAL SECTION: Lk 9:51-18:14.

We have now arrived—without too much confusion, I hope—at Lk's Special Section which runs from #137-186. What we find here are fifty paragraphs of which thirty-four are paralleled in Mt (probable Q material, therefore) but of which relatively little is found in Mk. This can be seen by noting the visible parallels to Lk (col. 3) found in col. 4 (Mt, but in a different context). There are sixteen paragraphs containing material which is uniquely Lukan (''L''). These are

#137 - The Samaritan Villagers
#144 - The Good Samaritan
#145 - Mary and Martha
#147 - The Friend at Midnight
#151 - The Blessedness of Jesus' Mother
#156 - Parable of the Rich Fool
#159 - The Servant's Wages
#162 - Repentance or Destruction
#163 - Healing of Woman with Spirit of Infirmity
#166 - Departure from Galilee
#173 - Prodigal Son
#175 - Hypocrisy of the Pharisees
#177 - Rich Man and Lazarus
#181 - The Servant's Wages
#182 - Healing of Ten Lepers (Grateful Samaritan)
#185 - Parable of the Unjust Judge

Lk's Special Section, therefore, is almost entirely Q + L, and completely independent of Mk. This fact has led some scholars to believe in the one-time existence of a Proto-Luke, an original edition of written material to which, as Lk's Gospel came into its present definitive version, large parts of Mk were added. This would account both for Lk's frequent dependence on Mk, in both sequence and content, and his considerable independence from him. According to this theory of a Proto-Luke, Lk has inserted between #130 = Mk 9:38-41 and #188 = Mk 10:13-16 a whole block of Lukan material which had already been cast into written form.

The sixteen paragraphs unique to Lk contain a fair number of references to Samaritans (#137, 144, 182), as will his Acts of the Apostles, and to women (#145, 151, 163, latter half of #172, 185). They also contain some of the most beautiful passages in the whole of the New Testament. One need think only of the Good Samaritan (#144), Mary and Martha (#145), and the Prodigal Son (#173).

This whole section is mainly teaching, framed within a journey narrative. Over a literary extension which moves from ch. 9 to ch. 18, it accompanies Jesus from the north in Galilee down to the outskirts of Jerusalem and its Temple. This is Jesus' journey as pilgrim-victim up to Jerusalem where he will celebrate the Christian work of salvation, the Christian exodus. (Cf. Lk 9:31 where the English translation "departure" masks the Greek original "exodus" which lies beneath it.) This pilgrimage motif is kept visible by Lk's occasional references to the journey which Jesus is making (Lk 9:51,53,56,57; 10:1; 13:22,33-34; 17:11) before he reaches Jericho (#193-194), Bethpage and Bethany (#196), and finally enters the Jerusalem temple (#198). But by this time Lk has at last rejoined Mk and Mt (#188) after having moved away from Mk following the sequence that extended from #122-130.

The bottom of p. xxiii, the whole of xxiv, and the top of xxv are, then, a *visible* demonstration of Lk's most striking and memorable literary phenomenon, a large section of about ten chapters (9:51-18:14) set in the middle of his Gospel, a sequence which depends entirely on himself and shows no influence from the Gospel of Mk.

III. THE JUDEAN SECTION

This section which includes the rest of the three gospels, exclusive of the resurrection appearances, is one in which the Synoptics are in close synchronization. It is universally accepted as the oldest organized extensive narrative in both Christian oral tradition and in Christian writing as well. It is easy, and logical, to imagine that a description of Jesus' final days in Jerusalem, just preceding and including his death, was a felt requirement for Christian worship. Jews came together to recall their exodus story; Christian Jews recalled, too, their particularly Christian exodus story, that of the raising up of Jesus on the cross and of his subsequent rising from the tomb.

It is at this point in the Jesus-story that it becomes possible also to include the evangelist John's description of Jesus' passion and death as parallel material. The fact that John's Gospel, so fundamentally different from the Synoptics, can be paralleled to the other three during the passion narrative indicates how quickly the *basic* story of Jesus' passion and death had been formalized, and how extensively it had spread through the various Christian communities.

A. THE JOURNEY TO JERUSALEM (#187-195).

Our eyes tell us that the three gospels are pretty much together. All of Mk is shared by at least one of the others. Mt has a special paragraph at #190. Lk has two at #194-195. But the section itself is easy enough to figure out. #187, Marriage and Divorce, disappears in Lk because he has already used this in his Special Section back at #176. He also cannot indicate, as do Mt and Mk in this paragraph, that Jesus is just now beginning the journey from Galilee down into Judea. For Lk this journey has already been in progress for ten chapters.

With #188, Jesus Blesses the Children, *all three* are back together for the first time since Lk broke ranks at 9:51 (#137). Mt adds the parable of the laborers in the vineyard (#190) which he considers suitable to the critical period into which Jesus' life is now moving. Lk omits #192, Jesus and the Sons of Zebedee, because it reflects so poorly on James and John. And he adds both #194, probably because his own "L" source located this story at Jericho, and #195, perhaps because the Parable of the Pounds seemed to contrast well with the good use that Zacchaeus made of his money while, at the same time, preparing the reader for the tragic story which was even now beginning to unfold, and which would lead to the death of Jesus and the destruction of Jerusalem.

B. THE DAYS IN JERUSALEM (#196-213).

This is another section which the three evangelists generally share, both in content and sequence. Again, everything in Mk is shared by at least one of the other two, and usually by both. Mt has added a bit, mainly in preparation for the great eschatological (final days) sermon which he is soon to present. Thus we find #203, the Parable of the Two Sons; #205, the Parable of the Marriage Feast; #211, The Lament over Jerusalem.

It would appear that he has dropped out the Cleansing of the Temple (#200), but this is not so. He has simply advanced it to #198 and made the cursing of the fig tree (#199) follow the cleansing and occur immediately. Mk's sequence is different. He makes the cursing of the fig tree (#199) into an initial statement, follows it with the cleansing of the temple (#200) and only later—the next morning—with the discovery of the withered tree (#201). Mk has thus sandwiched the temple cleansing between the two-act cursing of the fig tree, a device meant to show that the temple would be radically purified through destruction because, like the fig tree, it yielded no fruit. Lk, on his part, omits #199 completely, perhaps because he has a parable similar to it back at 13:6-9 (#162).

Mt omits #212, the Widow's Gift, perhaps because it does not appeal to him as suitable to the atmosphere of tragedy which is building up. The only paragraph which Lk adds to Mk is #197, The Destruction of *Jerusalem,* an element of Lukan insistence to deemphasize the expectation of the end of the world which was common to Christians of the early Church. Not the world, but Jerusalem, would be destroyed. The only other change he makes in the Markan material is the elimination of #208, the Great Commandment which he has already presented back in #143 as part of his Special Section.

THE SYNOPTIC APOCALYPSE (#214-230).

Here is another section not difficult to analyze, almost at sight. Every bit of Mk's material has been used here by both Mt and Lk except for #222, Mk's Ending to the Discourse which Mt uses later in #225, #228, and — in the case of Lk — #217, The Culmination of the Troubles, which Lk has already employed in ch. 17 (cf. col. 6). Lk has changed Mk's ending (#222) to an ending of his own (#223 and 230). His #230 is especially interesting since he paints a picture of Jesus who *every day* takes over the *temple* to teach the people. Jesus, just before death, has returned to his Father's house (Lk. 2:49).

By this time it should be evident to all of us what Mt is up to. He uses all of Mk's material but then adds to it statements and parables which he thinks suitable for this *fifth and last* of Jesus' great sermons, the Eschatological Discourse. This means—and is visibly evident on pp. xxv (at the bottom) and xxvi (the top)—that Mt has judged apropos to add on to Mk the following: #218, The Day of the Son of Man: #224, The Need for Watchfulness; #225, The Watchful Householder; #226, The Faithful and Wise Servant; #227, The Parable of the Ten Maidens; #228, The Parable of the Talents. Most of this material can be found also in Lk (cf. col. 6), but Mt has preferred to locate it at this point to build up the Sermon. And, as a splendid conclusion to this Sermon which for Mt marks the end and culmination of Jesus' teachings, Mt inserts #229, his magnificent description of the Last Judgment. Mt moves from it in #231 with his customary formula, but now significantly changed, to indicate that Jesus' teachings have now come to an end: "When Jesus had finished *all* these sayings . . ." (Mt. 26:1).

C. THE PASSION NARRATIVE.

The prelude to the Last Supper (#231-234) is found in our three gospels, and in order, except that Lk omits #232, The Anointing at Bethany. Now this is interesting since Lk, and only Lk, has a similar anointing—by a sinful woman—in 7:36-50 which he employs to demonstrate God's wisdom in choosing as Jesus' friends "tax collectors and sinners" (Lk. 7:34-35). The stories are so similar—perhaps from an identical origin—that Lk felt obliged to drop this Markan version.

THE LAST SUPPER (#235-253).

Here again the three columns almost match. All of Mk is found in both Mt and Lk except that Lk omits #247, the Mocking by the Soldiers. There may be two reasons for this. The first is that the story is a cruel one with its crown of thorns, its striking and spitting. Lk is adverse to cruelty. The second is that Lk has already described a somewhat similar contemptuous treatment given Jesus by Herod in #245, a passage lacking in both Mk and Mt.

Mt has added to Mk The Death of Judas (#243) and The Guard at the Tomb (#252), both bits of "M" material found in neither Mk nor Lk. Lk, too, has added a block of material all organized in the G.P. under #237 as Jesus' Last Words. But only the last four verses, vv. 35-38, The Two Swords, are not found in substance somewhere in the other two evangelists. The only other uniquely Lukan passage is #245, Jesus before Herod. Lk's reference to "Johanna, the wife of Chuza, Herod's steward" in 8:3 may give evidence of both his special interest and special source regarding Herod and his family.

Our parallels end with #253, The Empty Tomb. All three evangelists speak of a similar situation and event, but with striking differences in time, angels, women, angelic message, and reactions. Yet even here Mt is very close to Mk with the exception of a forceful change he makes as Mk, v. 8 becomes Mt, vv. 8-10. Lk, while telling basically the same story, is careful to reconstruct his own v. 6 so that the reader will not expect, nor even think of Galilean appearances of the risen Lord. Lk has strong theological reasons for wanting his Gospel story to end in Jerusalem. From there, from Jerusalem, it will go out to the ends of the world—but that will be the story of his other book, *The Acts of the Apostles*.

The final notation in the Index of the G.P. is captioned APPEARANCES OF THE RISEN LORD. The parallels have disappeared, just as they were non-existent for the opening infancy narratives of Mt and Lk. The resurrection narratives cannot be paralleled, should not be harmonized. Our index simply states that visually. Here, as we will see in later chapters, the theology of Mt and Lk take over. Mt's ending is a deep look into the theology (God-meaning) of his whole Gospel. Lk's ending serves the same purpose.

Chapter Four

Individual Sections of the Gospel Parallels: Emerging Personal Characteristics of the Evangelists

The Basic Technique

    With this chapter we pass from a consideration of the Index, with its emphasis on *sequence,* to the *content* of the gospel paragraphs themselves. What I intend to do here is to initiate the reader(s) into a technique designed to illuminate both the identities and dissimilarities in content which exist between our three gospel writers. A number of exemplars in graphic form will be offered to illustrate the method being followed, but the main work, the most important and rewarding work, will be done by you, the reader. Ordinarily I would ask students to work with different colored pencils at this task, but since the illustrations in this book will be in black and white, an even simpler technique will be used. Application will, I believe, make the method quite easy, but even this initial presentation should not be difficult to follow.

    1. The individual parts of Mk which are found duplicated in either Mt or Lk should be underlined in both Mk and the other evangelist. Whatever in Mk is shared by *both* Mt and Lk should be underlined twice in all three Synoptics. A sharing of successive words takes a continuous line. Identical, but separated words, have separated lines. Often successive words in Mk are found in the same order in Mt, for example, demanding a continuous line in both, but broken up in Lk. This means that the second underline is broken. Take, for example, a bit of #10 at the bottom of p. 15:

| But Jesus said to them, "A prophet is not without honor except in his own country and in his own house." 58 And he did not do many mighty works there, because of their unbelief. | 4 And Jesus said to them, "A prophet is not without honor, except in his own country, and among his own kin, and in his own house." 5 And he could do no mighty work there, except that he laid his hands upon a few sick people and healed them. 6 And he marveled because of their unbelief. | 24 And he said, "Truly, I say to you, no prophet is acceptable in his own country. |

In the first line "Jesus said to them" is underlined once with a continuous line since these words occur in exact succession in both Mt and Mk. The "said" gets an extra line in Mt and Mk since it occurs also in Lk where it, too, is twice underlined. In lines two and three "A prophet is not without honor except in his own country and" gets a single unbroken line since it is found in succession in both Mt and Mk. Lk concurs only with "prophet is" and "in his own country" so these get double lines in all three texts. At this point Lk disappears as a point of comparison and we can concentrate on Mk and Mt. In lines four and five Mk and Mt share in succession (unbroken line) "in his own house. And he . . ." In lines five and six we find only smaller bits to underline: thus, "do," "mighty work(s) there." The end of this section gives us Mk and Mt with an identical conclusion "because of their unbelief" to underline.

This is the simple technique to use for comparing material shared by all three. It is a time consuming process and, at times, might prove boring, but there is no substitute for this type of work if one wants to subject the inner relationships of the Synoptic Gospels to a rigorous examination and acquire an experienced feeling of their sameness, as also of the uniqueness of each. I would advise that the whole of the G.P. be worked over in this fashion, but will actually ask that only the exemplars which I will offer be redone by the readers for themselves, plus some other paragraphs which will be requested of the readers without exemplars to fall back on.

2. The second part of this marking technique concerns identities between Mt and Lk, sometimes when Mk is present, far more frequently when Mk is completely absent. These latter instances are usually examples of the Q sayings-material which both Mt and Lk have added—each in his own way—to Mk's Gospel. Presuming that we are not changing colors—as our exemplars do not—the idea is to place all identical words or phrases shared by Mt and Lk within parentheses. These parentheses will be long or short depending on the existence of shared phrases or sentences, or simply on the presence of individual identical words. Our first exampler, #2, will show you how this type of material should be handled.

2. JOHN'S PREACHING OF REPENTANCE

Matt. 3:7-10	Luke 3:7-9
7 But when he saw many of the Pharisees and Sadducees coming for baptism, he said to them, ("You brood of vipers! Who warned you to flee from the wrath to come? 8 Bear	7 He said therefore to the multitudes that came out to be baptized by him, ("You brood of vipers! Who warned you to flee from the wrath to come? 8 Bear

fruit)(that befits repentance, ⁹ and do not) presume (to say to yourselves, 'We have Abraham as our father'; for I tell you, God is able from these stones to raise up children to Abraham. ¹⁰ Even now the axe is laid to the root of the trees; every tree therefore that does not bear good fruit is cut down and thrown into the fire.")ʸ

fruits (that befit repentance, and do not) begin to say (to yourselves, 'We have Abraham as our father'; for I tell you, God is able from these stones to raise up children to Abraham. ⁹ Even now the axe is laid to the root of the trees; every tree therefore that does not bear good fruit is cut down and thrown into the fire.")ʸ

This is a remarkable example of our conjectured Q source. This long quotation (sixty-three Greek words in Mt, sixty-four in Lk) is word for word the same in our translation except that Mt's "fruit that befits" in verse 8 becomes "fruits that befit" in Lk, that Mt's "presume" is "begin" in Lk, and that Lk has one extra Greek *kai* which means "and." It is of some importance that this first occurrence of Q material is found as part of a Baptist sermon. It may well have been that the original Q collection began with a presentation of the Baptist. The introductions to the saying differ in both Mt and Lk because the saying itself originally had no introduction. Those found in Mt and Lk were created to fit the saying into context.

3. This method can intimidate the scrupulous in their attempt to get all the underlining and parentheses absolutely exact. Relax. In case of doubt, just move along to cases which seem very clear. A little experience will soon reduce doubts to a bare minimum.

4. Stop frequently in the comparisons of Mt-Mk-Lk to analyze for yourself which evangelist—if any—appears to be used by the others. My own belief, of course, is that Mt and Lk are using Mk. What does your experience say?

5. Note in the margins (side, top, bottom) or in the free spaces within the pages, material which is uniquely Matthean (M) or Lukan (L). And begin to write into these same spaces your own personal observations. The exemplars which follow will give you examples of some of the observations which I have added to my own copy of the G.P. over the years. The G.P. is, I suggest, a workbook. It becomes mine and yours only to the extent that our own additions to it begin to make it our own creation. For myself, as well as for you, I hope this will be a life-long rewarding task. One final caution: try to be neat. Writing all over a book, in any which way, can eventually obscure both the text and your personal reflections. Add only what you think has some importance . . . and do this in your best hand.

6. Any reader who, after studying through the underlining method recommended here, can devise one which works out better is free to go ahead with it. The details of such a revised method should be written out, step by step, within the front cover of the individual's G.P.

EXEMPLARS:

#2. John's Preaching of Repentance is found above.

6. THE BAPTISM OF JESUS.

Matt. 3:13–17	Mark 1:9–11	Luke 3:21–22
13 Then Jesus came from Galilee to the Jordan to John, to be baptized by him. 14 John would have prevented him, saying, "I need to be baptized by you, and do you come to me?" 15 But Jesus answered him, "Let it be so now; for thus it is fitting for us to fulfil all righteousness." Then he consented.	9 In those days Jesus came from Nazareth of Galilee	21 Now when all the people were baptized
16 And when Jesus was baptized, he went up immediately from the water, and behold, the heavens were opened and he saw the Spirit of God descending like a dove and alighting on him; 17 and lo, a voice from heaven, saying, "This is my beloved Son,ᵃ with whom I am well pleased."	and was baptized by John in the Jordan. 10 And when he came up out of the water, immediately he saw the heavens opened and the Spirit descending upon him like a dove; 11 and a voice came from heaven, "Thou art my beloved Son;ᵃ with thee I am well pleased."	and when Jesus also had been baptized and was praying, the heaven was opened, 22 and the Holy Spirit descended upon him in bodily form, as a dove, and a voice came from heaven, "Thou art my beloved Son;ᵃ with thee I am well pleased." ᵇ

Observations:

a) In Mt's account the initial verses insist on the Baptist's inferiority to Jesus, as also on Jesus' wish that all righteousness be fulfilled. This indicates that Mt's community is somewhat concerned about the relationship of the Baptist to Jesus, as also about the notion of "righteousness" which, for a Jewish community, must be related essentially to the observance of the Mosaic Law.

b) The most striking difference in the accounts is that in Lk's version John the Baptist disappears from view. In #5, the preceding paragraph in the G.P., Lk has mentioned John's imprisonment. As a result, even though Lk knows that John actually baptized Jesus, the Baptist himself is not mentioned. In fact, what is emphasized in Lk is not the baptism, but Jesus' *prayer* followed by the descent of the *Holy Spirit.* Both *prayer* and the *Holy Spirit,* and the relationship between the two, are strong Lukan themes.

c) The final quotation, speaking of Jesus as God's beloved son in whom the Father is well pleased, refers to Ps 2:7 and to Is 42:1.

d) The dove mentioned in all three texts may be an echo of Noah's dove (Gen. 8:8-12), and a figure of the new covenant after Jesus' *water* immersion.

8. THE TEMPTATION.

Matt. 4:1–11	Mark 1:12–13	Luke 4:1–13

1 Then (Jesus)

(was led) up (by the Spirit) into the wilderness to be (tempted by the devil.) 2 And he fasted forty days and forty nights and afterward (he was hungry.)

12 The Spirit immediately drove him out into the wilderness. 13 And he was in the wilderness forty days, tempted by Satan;

and he was with the wild beasts;

1 And (Jesus,) full of the Holy Spirit, returned from the Jordan, and (was led)(by the Spirit) 2 for forty days in the wilderness, (tempted by the devil.) And he ate nothing in those days; and when they were ended, (he was hungry.)

3 And the tempter came and (said to him, "If you are the Son of God, command these stones (to become) loaves of (bread.") 4 But he (answered,) ("It is written, 'Man shall not live by bread alone,) but by every word that proceeds from the mouth of God.' "

5 Then the devil (took him to) the holy city, (and set him on the pinnacle of the temple, 6 and said to him, "If you are the Son of God, throw yourself down,)(for it is written, 'He will give his angels charge of you,') (and 'On their hands they will bear you up, lest you strike your foot against a stone.' ") 7 (Jesus) said to (him,) "Again (it is) written, ('You shall not tempt the Lord your God.' ")

8 Again, (the devil took him) to a very high mountain, (and showed him all the kingdoms of the world) and the (glory) of them; 9 and he (said to him,) ("All) these (I will give)(you)

(if you) will fall down and (worship me.") 10 Then (Jesus) said to (him,) "Begone, Satan! for (it is written, 'You shall worship the Lord your God, and him only shall you serve.' ")

3 The devil (said to him, "If you are the Son of God, command this stone) (to become)(bread.") 4 And Jesus (answered) him, ("It is written, 'Man shall not live by bread alone.' ")

cf. vv. 9–12

5 And (the devil took him) up, (and showed him all the kingdoms of the world) in a moment of time, 6 and (said to him,) "To (you)(I will give)(all) this authority and their (glory;) for it has been delivered to me, and I give it to whom I will. 7 (If you,) then, will (worship me,) it shall all be yours." 8 And (Jesus) answered (him,) ("It is written, 'You shall worship the Lord your God, and him only shall you serve.' ")

9 And he (took him to) Jerusalem, (and set him on the pinnacle of the temple, and said to him, "If you are the Son of God, throw yourself down) from here; 10 (for it is written, 'He will give his angels charge of you,) to guard you,' 11 (and 'On their hands they will bear you up, lest you strike your foot against a stone.' ") 12 And (Jesus) answered (him,) ("It is) said, ('You shall not tempt the Lord your God.' ")

cf. vv. 5–7

¹¹ Then (the devil) left him, and behold, <u>angels</u> came and <u>ministered to him.</u>	and the <u>angels ministered to him.</u>	¹³ And when (the devil) had ended every temptation, he departed from him until an opportune time.

Observations:

a) <u>Mk's account</u> is very simple. Nothing at all is said <u>with regard to specific temptations.</u> For this reason the Markan column disappears almost immediately, to reappear only at the very end of the text.

b) <u>The specific temptations</u> are the same, and in almost identical language, <u>in both Mt and L</u>k. Our <u>presumption is that both</u> found the story written in such similar detail <u>in their common source, Q.</u> You will notice that, although the story is narrative in form, its main <u>force comes from its sayings.</u> The most striking difference between the two is that the temple-Jerusalem temptation appears in second place in Mt, but in third place in Lk. My own guess is that <u>Lk has shifted the position</u> so that the temptation story, like Lk's Gospel itself, <u>will end in Jerusalem.</u>

c) It is interesting to see how <u>Mt,</u> though so very independent of Mk in this account, <u>returns to the Markan text to repeat that</u> "angels . . . ministered to him."

d) It is difficult to use the underlining-parentheses technique in the triple opening of the story. Both Mt and Lk seem to be influenced not only by their common source, Q, but also by Mk's version. One can see Mk's influence in Mt's <u>"into the wilderness"</u> and Lk's <u>"forty days in the wilderness."</u> Verses like these should not overly disturb the reader. We can do little more here than guess at the exact influence which both Mk and Q had on the texts of Mt and Lk at this precise point.

e) The <u>Old Testament quotations</u> with which Jesus responds to the tempter <u>are all</u> <u>from the Book of Deuteronomy.</u> Certainly one of the teachings of both Mt and Lk at this point is that <u>Jesus, the true Israel, conquers in the desert wilderness</u> the <u>temptations</u> which overcame the Old Testament Israel.

10. THE REJECTION AT NAZARETH.

Matt. 13:54–58 (§ *108, p. 76*)	Mark 6:1–6a (§ *108, p. 76*)	Luke 4:16–30
54 And coming <u>to his own country</u> <u>he</u> taught them <u>in</u> their <u>synagogue,</u>	1 <u>He</u> went away from there and came <u>to his own country;</u> and his disciples followed him. ² And <u>on the sabbath</u> <u>he</u> began to <u>teach in the synagogue;</u>	16 And <u>he came</u> to Nazareth, where he had been brought up; and <u>he</u> went to <u>the synagogue,</u> as <u>his</u> custom was, <u>on the sabbath</u> day. And he stood up to read; ¹⁷ and there was given to him the book of the prophet Isaiah. He opened the book, and found the place where it was written, ¹⁸ "The Spirit of the Lord is upon me, because he has anointed me to preach good news to the poor. He has sent me to proclaim release to the captives and recovering of

so that they were astonished,

and said, "Where did this man get this wisdom and these mighty works? ⁵⁵ Is not this the carpenter's (son?) Is not his mother called Mary? And are not his brothers James and Joseph and Simon and Judas? ⁵⁶ And are not all his sisters with us? Where then did this man get all this?" ⁵⁷ And they took offense ^e at him.

But Jesus said to them, "A prophet is not without honor except in his own country and in his own house." ⁵⁸ And he did not do many mighty works there,

because of their unbelief.

and many who heard him were astonished,

saying, "Where did this man get all this? What is the wisdom given to him? What mighty works are wrought by his hands! ³ Is not this the carpenter, the son of Mary and brother of James and Joses and Judas and Simon, and are not his sisters here with us? And they took offense ^e at him.

⁴ And Jesus said to them, "A prophet is not without honor, except in his own country, and among his own kin, and in his own house." ⁵ And he could do no mighty work there, except that he laid his hands upon a few sick people and healed them. ⁶ And he marveled because of their unbelief.

sight to the blind, to set at liberty those who are oppressed, ¹⁹ to proclaim the acceptable year of the Lord." ²⁰ And he closed the book, and gave it back to the attendant, and sat down; and the eyes of all in the synagogue were fixed on him. ²¹ And he began to say to them, "Today this scripture has been fulfilled in your hearing." ²² And all spoke well of him, and wondered at the gracious words which proceeded out of his mouth; and they said,

"Is not this Joseph's (son?)"

²³ And he said to them, "Doubtless you will quote to me this proverb, 'Physician, heal yourself; what we have heard you did at Capernaum, do here also in your own country.'" ²⁴ And he said, "Truly, I say to you, no prophet is acceptable in his own country.

²⁵ But in truth, I tell you, there were many widows in Israel in the days of Elijah, when the heaven was shut up three years and six months, when there came a great famine over all

the land; 26 and Elijah was sent to none of them but only to Zarephath, in the land of Sidon, to a woman who was a widow. 27 And there were many lepers in Israel in the time of the prophet Elisha; and none of them was cleansed, but only Naaman the Syrian." 28 When they heard this, all in the synagogue were filled with wrath. 29 And they rose up and put him out of the city, and led him to the brow of the hill on which their city was built, that they might throw him down headlong. 30 But passing through the midst of them he went away.

Observations:

a) Lk has advanced this passage about Jesus' inaugural address at Nazareth (ch. 4 in Lk, ch. 6 in Mk, ch. 13 in Mt) and enlarged it for reasons which we shall see in just a moment.

b) At the very beginning of the passage Mt is closer to Mk than is Lk, except for the latter's "on the sabbath" which is missing in Mt.

c) In the center of the passage Mt follows Mk very closely. His major change is to revise Mk's "son of Mary" since family identification is traced through the father. Lk seems to feel this difficulty also. So Mt identifies Jesus as "the carpenter's son" while Lk calls him "Joseph's son."

d) Mt, again, is very similar to Mk's vv. 4-6. Yet even here he has made two clear changes. He has dropped Mk's "among his own kin," perhaps to soften what seems to be an aspersion on Jesus' own family. (Lk drops the reference to both "kin" and "house.") Mt has also had difficulty with Mk's statement that Jesus "*could* do no mighty work there." This incapacity has been avoided by Mt's change to "he *did* not do many mighty works there." These are two clear instances in which it is easy to see why and how Mt changed Mk, but it would be difficult to imagine that Mk changed the milder and less difficult text of Mt.

e) This is a passage in which, through the comparison with Mk and Mt, we can see Lk at work. He has advanced Jesus' Rejection at Nazareth from the later position it has in the sequence of both Mk and Mt, even though this means a mention in v. 23 of miracles done at Capernaum even before Lk ever locates Jesus in that city (cf. Lk 4:31). Lk has a profound theological purpose to this shift. He wishes to present at the very beginning of Jesus' ministry a preview of his life story. His mission is announced by Lk in vv. 18-19 as the fulfillment of the beautiful liberation passages of Is 61:1-2; 58:6.

This announcement is next followed briefly by initial success (v. 22) and then of mounting hostility (vv. 23-28). The story concludes with threat of death on a hill outside of the city. This Lukan passage is a well-designed overture to the whole gospel story of Jesus' life. And, in fact, it is more than that. It even begins to prepare the reader for Lk's second volume, the Acts of the Apostles, with its extension of salvation to the Gentiles. The Elijah and Elisha incidents of vv. 25-27 in which salvation is carried to a woman by Elijah through bread, and to a man by Elisha through water, are an advance notice of the days in which salvation in Jesus' name will be brought to all—men, women, and Gentiles—through the Church's own Eucharistic bread and baptismal water. What we are privileged to see here is Lk's creative genius at work. A similarly striking display of Lk's creativity is apparent also in the exemplar that follows.

11. THE CALL OF THE FIRST DISCIPLES.

Matt. 4:18–22	Mark 1:16–20	
18 As he walked by the Sea of Galilee, he saw two brothers, Simon who is called Peter and Andrew his brother, casting a net into the sea; for they were fishermen. 19 And he said to them, "Follow me, and I will make you fishers of men." 20 Immediately they left their nets and followed him.	16 And passing along by the Sea of Galilee he saw Simon and Andrew the brother of Simon casting a net into the sea; for they were fishermen. 17 And Jesus said to them, "Follow me, and I will make you become fishers of men." 18 And immediately they left their nets and followed him.	*cf. 5:1–11* (§ 17, *p. 19*)
21 And going on from there he saw two other brothers, James the son of Zebedee and John his brother, in the boat with Zebedee their father, mending their nets, and he called them. 22 Immediately they left the boat and their father, and followed him. (*4:23 f. p. 18*)	19 And going on a little farther, he saw James the son of Zebedee and John his brother, who were in their boat mending the nets. 20 And immediately he called them, and they left their father Zebedee in the boat with the hired servants, and followed him.	

17. THE MIRACULOUS CATCH OF FISH.

Luke 5:1–11

(*cf. Mark 1:16–20 and Matt. 4:18–22, § 11, p. 16*)

1 While the people pressed upon him to hear the word of God, he was standing by the lake of Gennesaret. 2 And he saw two boats by the lake; but the fishermen had gone out of them and were washing their nets. 3 Getting into one of the boats, which was Simon's, he asked him to put out a little from the land. And he sat down and taught the people from the boat.*** 4 And when he had ceased speaking, he said to Simon, "Put out into the deep and let down your nets for a catch." 5 And Simon answered, "Master, we toiled all night and took nothing! But at your word I will let down the nets." 6 And when they had done this, they enclosed a great shoal of fish; and as their nets were breaking, 7 they beckoned to their partners in the other boat to come and help them. And they came and filled both the boats, so that they began to sink. 8 But when Simon Peter saw it, he fell down at Jesus' knees, saying, "Depart from me, for I am a sinful man, O Lord." 9 For he was astonished, and all that were

with him, at the catch of fish which they had taken; [10] and so also were James and John, sons of Zebedee, who were partners with Simon. And Jesus said to Simon, "Do not be afraid; henceforth you will be catching men." [11] And when they had brought their boats to land, they left everything and followed him. *(5:12–16, § 45, pp. 31–32.)*

Observations:

a) These two sections, #11 and 17, are essentially the same story. That of Mk and Mt has been expanded by Lk as will become apparent.

b) The texts of Mk and Mt are almost identical. Mt's changes are slight and insignificant. Perhaps he adds the clause "who is called Peter" simply because—as we shall see later—Peter, the rock (cf. Mt 16:18), is extremely important for Mt and for his community.

c) The impressive change comes when we turn to the same story as told by Lk in #17. The basics in all three accounts are the same. Jesus calls Simon and his partner (unnamed in Lk, vv. 6-7), plus James and John, sons of Zebedee, by the Sea of Galilee = Lake of Gennesaret. He announces to Simon that he will in the future catch men. Then, in Lk as in Mk-Mt, they leave all and follow Jesus. But Lk has extensively reworked this account by inserting into it the exemplifying story of the miraculous catch. In so doing, Lk reveals himself as an excellent preacher. He has exemplified for his audience (preached to, originally, and now being addressed in writing) what it means to be Christian "fishers of men." Without Christ one would fish all night and catch nothing; with Christ's presence, the catch will be almost immeasurable. This story which Lk has used to concretize the abstract "fishers of men" bears striking resemblance to a similar account in the final chapter of John's Gospel, and is probably to be identified with it. Lk could not use it as a post-resurrection story since his Gospel ends, and must end, in Jerusalem and not back north at the Sea of Galilee. So, good preacher that he is, he has made brilliant use of it here. Note the centrality of Simon Peter in Lk's account as in Jn 21. And consider how poignant Simon's "Depart from me, for I am a sinful man, O Lord" becomes if this story originally concerned Peter's encounter with his risen Lord shortly after his triple denial during the passion.

13. THE HEALING OF PETER'S MOTHER-IN-LAW.

Matt. 8:14–15 (§ 47, p. 33)	Mark 1:29–31	Luke 4:38–39
14 And when Jesus entered Peter's house,	29 And immediately he left the synagogue, and entered the house of Simon and Andrew, with James and John. 30 Now Simon's	38 And he arose and left the synagogue, and entered Simon's house.
he saw his mother-in-law lying sick with a fever;	mother-in-law lay sick with a fever, and immediately they told him of her. 31 And he came	Now Simon's mother-in-law was ill with a high fever, and they besought him for her.
15 and he touched her hand, and the fever left her, and (she rose) and served him.	and took her by the hand and lifted her up, and the fever left her; and she served them.	39 And he stood over her and rebuked the fever, and it left her; and immediately (she rose) and served them.

Observations:

a) This is a typical miracle story. Simon's mother-in-law is sick with a fever. Jesus acts upon her. She is cured and serves the small group. This seems to be a purely historical remembrance passed along by Peter. The story contains nothing to give it a theological teaching for the readers unless it be—and this is almost too nuanced—that those touched by the Lord's blessing should respond with service.

b) The text in all three is very similar. Mt has abbreviated—as is his custom—and, in so doing, has focused all attention on Jesus until the final line in which the cured woman rises and serves.

c) There is an unusual literary correspondence in the final verse between Mt and Lk who use the phrase "she rose" which is not found in Mk except in the equivalent phrase "lifted him up." This identity between Mk and Lk is so brief and can have been so easily derived from the Markan equivalent that it cannot argue direct literary relationship between Mt and Lk.

d) It is interesting to note that Lk, in postponing the call of the first disciples from #11, as in Mk and Mt, to #17 presents Simon's mother-in-law before presenting Simon himself. This is a clear indication that Lk depends on another text (Mk's) with a different sequence.

The Sermon on the Mount.

Matthew 5–7

18. INTRODUCTION.

Matt. 5:1-2		Luke 6:12, 20 (§ 72, *p. 54;* § 73, *p. 55*)
1 Seeing the crowds,(he went) up on the mountain, and when he sat down(his disciples) came to him. 2 And he opened his mouth and taught them, saying:	*3:13*	6:12 In these days (he went) out into the hills to pray; and all night he continued in prayer to God. 20 And he lifted up his eyes on (his disciples,) and said:

19. THE BEATITUDES

Matt. 5:3-12		Luke 6:20-23 (§ 73, *p. 55*)
3 ("Blessed are)the(poor)in spirit, (for)theirs(is the kingdom of)heaven.		20("Blessed are)you(poor,) (for)yours(is the kingdom of)God.
4 "Blessed are those who mourn, for they shall be comforted.		
5 "Blessed are the meek, for they shall inherit the earth.		
6("Blessed are)those who (hunger)and thirst for righteousness, (for)they(shall be satisfied.)		21("Blessed are)you that(hunger)now, (for)you(shall be satisfied.) "Blessed are you that weep now, for you shall laugh.
7 "Blessed are the merciful, for they shall obtain mercy.		
8 "Blessed are the pure in heart, for they shall see God.		

9 "Blessed are the peacemakers,
  for they shall be called sons of God.
10 "Blessed are those who are persecuted
  for righteousness' sake,
  for theirs is the kingdom of heaven.
11("Blessed are you when men)
  (revile you)
and persecute you and utter all kinds of
(evil) against you falsely (on) my (account.)
  12(Rejoice) and be glad, (for)(your reward
is great in heaven, for so) men persecuted
(the prophets) who were before you.

22("Blessed are you when men) hate you,
and when they exclude you and (revile you)
and cast out your name as (evil,)(on)
(account) of the Son of man!
  23(Rejoice) in that day, and leap for
joy, (for) behold, (your reward is great in
heaven; for so) their fathers did to (the
prophets.")

74. THE WOES
Luke 6:24–26

24 "But woe to you that are rich, for you have received your consolation. 25 Woe to you that are full now, for you shall hunger. Woe to you that laugh now, for you shall mourn and weep. 26 Woe to you, when all men speak well of you, for so their fathers did to the false prophets.

Observations:

a) For Mt, this is the beginning of the Sermon on the Mount, a collection of Jesus' sayings that takes up chs. 5-7. It is situated on a mountain, to bring out a Jesus-Moses parallel, something which is obviously important for Mt and his community. The introductory verses in Lk are limited in our G.P. text to vv. 12 and 20 and are similar to Mt, but with a double Lukan insistence on prayer. What is not obvious is that in vv. 17-19 (cf. G.P., p. 53) Lk has Jesus come down from the mountain to "a level place" where he can meet and speak to the diseased and those in need of healing. Mt's Sermon on the Mount is Lk's Sermon on the Plain: Mt wishes to present Jesus as the new Moses, Lk wishes to present him ministering to and addressing the sick, for whom mountain climbing would hardly be a favorite sport.

b) Mt's version is in the third person, "Blessed are the . . . for they . . ." Lk's is in the second and speaks directly to the hearer and reader: "Blessed are you . . . for you . . ."

c) Mt's text is considerably longer so far as the beatitudes are concerned. Lk's is shorter in this regard, but has a striking parallelism which is completely lacking in Mt. Note how Lk balances each of the beatitudes with a corresponding woe, and each section with a corresponding conclusion:

poor (v. 20)	rich (v. 24)
hunger (v. 21)	full (v. 25)
weep (v. 21)	laugh (v. 25)
men hate you (v. 22)	men speak well of you (v. 26)
for so their fathers did to	for so their fathers did to
the prophets (v. 23)	the false prophets (v. 26).

d) As we consider these similar, but differing, passages in Mt and Lk it is hard to imagine that either one has a copy of the other. The differences are just too sharp. But they could both be working from written descriptions of a Jesus sermon whose content had changed in the course of translation, or whose content could have been influenced on the part of the evangelist by a differing oral version known to him. We might label this Q material, but Q with a difference. And Lk's ending, with its perfect parallelism, demands a great deal of creativity on the part of the evangelist, a creativity of which—as we have already seen—Lk is perfectly capable.

38. GOD'S ANSWERING OF PRAYER.

Matt. 7:7–11	Luke 11:9–13 (§ 148, p. 106)
"7 (Ask, and it will be given you; seek, and you will find; knock, and it will be opened to you. 8 For every one who asks receives, and he who seeks finds, and to him who knocks it will be opened.) 9 Or (what) man of (you, if his son asks him for) bread, will give him a stone? 10 Or if he asks for (a fish, will) (give him a serpent?) 11 (If you then, who are evil, know how to give good gifts to your children, how much more will) your (Father) who is in (heaven) (give) good things (to those who ask him!)	9 "And I tell you, (Ask, and it will be given you; seek, and you will find; knock, and it will be opened to you. 10 For every one who asks receives, and he who seeks finds, and to him who knocks it will be opened.) 11 (What) father among (you, if his son asks for c) (a fish, will) instead of a fish (give him a serpent;) 12 or if asks for an egg, will give him a scorpion? 13 (If you then, who are evil, know how to give good gifts to your children, how much more will) the (heavenly (Father) (give) the Holy Spirit (to those who ask him!")

Observations:

This is another example of a Jesus saying found only in Mt and Lk, another Q, therefore. Most of it is word for word the same in the two Gospels, but there is one significant difference. Note Lk's ending in which not "good things" but "the Holy Spirit" is given by the Father to those who ask him. This is a special Lukan touch, a pivotal point in this theology. Prayer is infallible, says Luke, because when you pray God's answer is always there in the form of the Spirit who is given to us. No prayer is ever unanswered.

113. THE WALKING ON THE WATER.

Matt. 14:22–33	Mark 6:45–52
22 Then he made the disciples get into the boat and go before him to the other side, while he dismissed the crowds. 23 And after he had dismissed the crowds, he went up into the hills by himself to pray.	45 Immediately he made his disciples get into the boat and go before him to the other side, to Bethsaida, while he dismissed the crowd. 46 And after he had taken leave of them, he went into the hills to pray.

When evening came, he was there alone, 24 but the boat by this time was many furlongs distant from the land,q beaten by the waves; for the wind was against them. 25 And in the fourth watch of the night he came to them, walking on the sea. 26 But when the disciples saw him walking on the sea, they were terrified, saying, "It is a ghost!" And they cried out for fear. 27 But immediately he spoke to them, saying, "Take heart, it is I; have no fear."

47 And when evening came, the boat was out on the sea, and he was alone on the land. 48 And he saw that they were distressed in rowing, for the wind was against them. And about the fourth watch of the night he came to them, walking on the sea. He meant to pass by them, 49 but when they saw him walking on the sea, they thought it was a ghost, and cried out; 50 for they all saw himr and were terrified. But immediately he spoke to them and said, "Take heart, it is I; have no fear."

28 And Peter answered him, "Lord, if it is you, bid me come to you on the water." 29 He said, "Come." So Peter got out of the boat and walked on the water and came to Jesus; 30 but when he saw the wind,s he was afraid, and beginning to sink he cried out, "Lord, save me." 31 Jesus immediately reached out his hand and caught him, saying to him, "O man of little faith, why did you doubt?" 32 And when they got into the boat, the wind ceased. 33 And those in the boat worshiped him, saying, "Truly you are the Son of God."

51 And he got into the boat with them and the wind ceased. And they were utterly astounded, 52 for they did not understand about the loaves, but their hearts were hardened.

Observations:

a) The most evident point here is that Lk is missing. If you will check back in the Index, xxiii, you will see that it is precisely at this point (#113) that Lk begins what we have called his Great Omission. Seemingly Lk is beginning to worry about saving space on the scroll for his own special section which will begin at #137. One way to do this is to eliminate stories which are similar to previous ones. Thus, the account of the second multiplication of the loaves (#118) will disappear in Lk. Probably #113 disappears here because it is so similar to #105, The Stilling of the Storm.

b) The accounts in Mk and Mt are very similar, so both texts end up heavily underlined. Yet there are also significant differences in Mt that allow us to hazard founded guesses as to what he has in mind. Mt's v. 24 places emphasis on the precarious situation of "the boat . . . beaten by the waves." Mk states things differently at this point. Perhaps the *boat* has a special significance for Mt.

c) Mt's vv. 28-31 are M material, unique to him. Peter ventures out onto the waters. With faith, all goes well; as soon as faith wavers, one begins to sink. Yet even then Jesus is there as savior to those who confess that "Truly you are the Son of God" (v. 33).

d) These Matthean peculiarities give reason to speculate that Mt has in mind his own community, a group passing through troubled days. It is a boat (a Christian symbol for the Church from the earliest days) shaken by the waves. But—and this the evangelist wishes to emphasize—there is no danger if one retains faith in the Son of God. Then, indeed, even walking on the troubled waters is possible.

e) Note the *amazing* difference between Mt's conclusion, "Truly you are the Son of God," and that of Mk for whom the disciples "were utterly astounded, for they did not understand about the loaves, but their hearts were hardened." The two conclusions just could not be more different. Mt's theology is going in one direction, Mk's in another. Mk—as we shall see—presents the first great profession of faith, that of Peter, two chapters later in 8:29. At this point in his story the disciples are still asking themselves the perplexing question, "Who then is this, that even wind and sea obey him?" (4:41).

f) The difference in conclusions is one example of an instance in which it is easy to imagine Mt having Mk's difficult text and changing it to a Christian profession of faith. But it is difficult to imagine Mk beginning with Mt's profession and changing it to what is almost a direct opposite. The dependency must be of Mt upon Mk and not vice versa. Our final example will scan

122. THE CONFESSION AT CAESAREA PHILIPPI AND THE FIRST PREDICTION OF THE PASSION.

Matt. 16.13–23	Mark 8:27–33	Luke 9:18–22
		(9:10–17, § 112, pp. 79–80)
13 Now when Jesus came into the district of Caesarea Philippi, he asked his disciples, "Who do men say that the Son of man is?"[1] 14 And they said, "Some say John the Baptist, others say Elijah, and others Jeremiah or one of the prophets." 15 (He said to them,) "But who do you say that I am?" 16 Simon Peter replied, "You are the Christ, the Son (of) the living (God.")	27 And Jesus went on with his disciples, to the villages of Caesarea Philippi; and on the way he asked his disciples, "Who do men say that I am?" 28 And they told him, "John the Baptist; and others say, Elijah; and others one of the prophets." 29 And he asked them, "But who do you say that I am?" Peter answered him, "You are the Christ."	18 Now it happened that as he was praying alone the disciples were with him;[j] and he asked them, "Who do the people say that I am?" 19 And they answered, "John the Baptist; but others say, Elijah; and others that one of the old prophets has risen." 20 And (he said to them,) "But who do you say that I am?" And Peter answered, "The Christ (of)(God.")
17 And Jesus answered him, "Blessed are you, Simon Bar-Jona! For flesh and blood has not revealed this to you, but my Father who is in heaven. 18 And I tell you, you are Peter,[k] and on this rock[l] I will build my church, and the powers of death[m] shall not prevail against it. 19 I will give you the		

keys of the kingdom of heaven, and whatever you bind on earth shall be bound in heaven, and whatever you loose on earth shall be loosed in heaven." *
20 Then he strictly charged the disciples to tell no one that he was the Christ.

21 From that time Jesus[n] began to show his disciples that he must go to Jerusalem and suffer many things from the elders and chief priests and scribes, and be killed, and (on the third day be raised.)

22 And Peter took him and began to rebuke him, saying, "God forbid, Lord! This shall never happen to you." 23 But he turned and said to Peter, "Get behind me, Satan! You are a hindrance[o] to me; for you are not on the side of God, but of men."

---

30 And he charged them to tell no one about him.
31 And he began to teach them that the Son of man must suffer many things, and be rejected by the elders and the chief priests and the scribes, and be killed, and after three days rise again.
32 And he said this plainly. And Peter took him, and began to rebuke him. 33 But turning and seeing his disciples, he rebuked Peter, and said, "Get behind me, Satan! For you are not on the side of God, but of men."

---

21 But he charged and commanded them to tell this to no one,

22 saying, "The Son of man must suffer many things, and be rejected by the elders and chief priests and scribes, and be killed, and (on the third day be raised.")

Observations:

a) Our underlining indicates, first of all, that the three texts are very similar. Yet the differences, even the small ones, are also striking.

b) Lk alone mentions that Jesus was *praying* (v. 18), a frequent Lukan touch. And Lk alone omits the rebuke of Peter in Mk's vv. 32-33. Lk is not one for delaying on, or even referring to, the faults of others. What might make people look bad will almost inevitably disappear in the Lukan text.

c) Peter's profession of faith is simplest in Mk, "You are the Christ"; a bit more specific in Lk, "The Christ of God"; most theological in Mt, "You are the Christ, the Son of the living God." Again, it is easier to imagine Lk, and especially Mt, adding to Mk rather than Mk subtracting from either of the other professions.

d) Only Mt has the heavily theological reference to Peter in his vv. 17-19. Obviously Peter must have been an extremely important personage to Mt and his community, a community which Mt extends out into a Church (v. 18) with power both on earth and in heaven. For this Church, Peter would be rock.

Conclusion:

The preceding examples have been offered in some detail to give you a feel for this type of comparative study, and to help you to appreciate the value of it. Sometimes it will seem that the underlining brings little to light, except perhaps to impress you with the similarities in the texts. At other times—and these are the moments of light and amazement—the differences in the texts, the things that Mt and Lk do to the Markan original, will take you right inside the evangelist's head and show you his creative genius and distinctive theology at work. It is with these moments of light in mind that I encourage you now to continue with this work on your own. The ideal would be to make your way through the whole G.P. This might take a couple of months, but it will be well worth the effort. At least take an honest try at the following sections which I will simply list with just a phrase or two to point out some aspect that might be well worth studying.

#30. The Lord's Prayer

a) Q material
b) Mt's vv. 14-15 found in different context in Mk.

#34. Serving Two Masters

a) Striking Q
b) Notice further Q material in #35-36 and #38-39.

#67. Jesus' Thanksgiving to the Father

a) Another excellent example of Q
b) Lukan characteristics seen in "rejoiced" and "Holy Spirit"

#69. Plucking Ears of Grain on Sabbath

a) Fine example of triple-tradition
b) Mt's addition in vv. 5-7 makes Jesus greater than the temple, the site of God's presence.
c) Puzzling elimination of Mk's v. 27 by both Mt and Lk

#87-88. Against Seeking for Signs. The Return of Evil Spirit

More of Q, much of it identical word for word.

#106. The Gerasene Demoniac

a) Similarity of Lk to Mk
b) Mt, as often, abbreviates.

#111. The Death of John

a) Lk disappears — story too brutal?
b) Mt abbreviates.

#125. The Coming of Elijah

a) Lk disappears—for him Jesus is *the* Elijah figure.
b) Mt's specification of John Baptist (v. 13) looks like addend to clarify Mk.

#143. The Lawyer's Question

a) Two laws in Mk; two in Mt, but second like first; only one in Lk
b) Unusual agreements of Mt and Lk in use of "lawyer . . . test . . . teacher"
c) Lk's insistence (v. 28) on *doing*

#192. *Jesus and Sons of Zebedee*

a) James and John make request in Mk, their mother in Mt. Request disappears in Lk.
b) Mt abbreviates Mk's difficult vv. 38-39.
c) Lk transfers discussion about service to Last Supper (Lk *22*:24-27).

#216. *The Desolating Sacrilege*

a) Mk's "desolating sacrilege" clarified by Mt, clarified further by Lk.
b) Mt's "on a sabbath" (v. 20) is a Jewish concern.
c) Mk's vv. 19-20 have unclear reference, copied by Mt, clarified by Lk.

#226. *Faithful and Wise Servant*

More of Q

#234. *Preparation for Passover*

a) Mt abbreviates
b) Lk's "Peter and John" (v. 8) specifies Mk's "two of his disciples" (v. 13).

#239. *Jesus in Gethsemane*

a) Mk and Mt very similar
b) Lk's greater emphasis on prayer in vv. 40, 44-45.
c) Lk's gentleness with apostles. He has them sleep only once, and "for sorrow."

#253. *The Empty Tomb*

a) Strong similarity between Mk and Mt till final verses
b) Mt's great earthquake (v. 2) and eschatological sign. New age has dawned.
c) Reference to future appearance in Galilee (v. 7 in Mk and Mt) is changed in Lk (v. 6) for whom Gospel story must conclude in Jerusalem.

Chapter Five

The Good News
According to Mark

The Gospel of Mark is Mk's vision of what the good news about Jesus meant to himself and to his community. In writing this small book Mark created a new type of literature. Not history, it contains historical elements; not drama, its cycle of successes and failures, of supreme tragedy and ultimate victory, is the stuff that dramatic masterpieces are made of; not biography, it presents a compelling picture of *The Man for Others* which has influenced the centuries; not a creed, it gives a profession of faith rooted in reality and challenging in acceptance; not liturgy, it yet contains elements both from and for Christian worship.

The trick with Mk—as will be true, too, of Mt and Lk—is to grasp clearly the author's main purpose, his main thrust and message. It is that which will provide the key for the reader's interpretation of the whole and its parts. This will be the main object of this chapter, not a verse-by-verse exposition of the Gospel, but an attempt to find the heart of the Gospel, the message which both inspired Mk to write his version of the Good News and which makes his version different from those of the other evangelists. The most important encouragement I can give you at this moment is to read and reread Mk, at times going through the whole Gospel at one sitting. There is no substitute for familiarity with the text.

1. Major Division

Every book written on Mk's Gospel will provide you with some kind of a division, and hardly any two will agree exactly with each other. The following, my own, is extremely general, pointing out the two main sections of the book. These are indicated, surprisingly, in the very first verse, in what seems to be Mk's title to the whole work: "The beginning of the gospel of Jesus <u>Christ, the Son of God</u>" (1:1). I have underlined the last five words because they are the creedal expressions, the professions of faith to which the Gospel leads. Jesus is both "Christ" (8:29) and "Son of God" (15:39). And that, simply enough, is the way the Gospel is divided. What I mean more explicitly is this:

Part One (1:1-8:29) stresses the mystery of Jesus' identity. The basic question to be answered by all who are interested in Jesus of Nazareth is, "Who then is this . . .?" (4:41). The question will be answered by Peter's words, "You are the *Christ*" (8:29), a confession which marks the turning point in the Gospel.

Part Two (8:30-16:8) carries Peter's initial profession to a much deeper level. "Christ," yes, but what kind of Christ, and what kind of disciple in his footsteps? This leads to the centurion's confession, "Truly this man was the *Son of God*" (15:39) and to the angel's confirming witness, "He has risen, he is not here; see the place where they laid him" (16:6). It is at this point that Mk's Gospel ends. What follows in 16:9-20 is an addition to the original account. The addition, however, is extremely old, found as it is in the second century writings of both Tatian and Irenaeus.

2. Mark's Purpose and Theology

a) Mk wishes to involve his reader in a gripping, existential, salvific drama. His purpose is to give his reader (Christian, near Christian, interested non-Christian) an opportunity to relive the life of Jesus' first disciples. His amazing use both of the present tense (151 times)—older American readers might think of the same mannerism in Damon Runyon—and of the adverb "immediately" help to draw his audience into the narrative action. It enables the reader to proceed as a participant with those first disciples to an initial confession of faith in Jesus as Christ (8:29), and then to a much more complete belief in him as Son of God (15:39). But this faith must be nuanced. Jesus is indeed Christ, but a suffering-Son of Man Christ; Jesus is indeed Son of God, but his divine sonship is most fully recognized in the moment of his supreme suffering and servanthood (15:39 in the light of 10:45). It is this overall purpose that controls Mk's presentation.

b) The initial profession of faith (8:29) is in Jesus as Christ. Mk prepares the reader for this by presenting a Jesus mighty in both word and work, and surprising in his claims.

His *word*, his doctrine, is a source of amazement. "And they were astonished at his teaching, for he taught them as one who had authority, and not as the scribes" (1:22). "And they were all amazed, so that they questioned among themselves, saying, 'What is this? A new teaching!' " (1:27) "And on the sabbath he began to teach in the synagogue; and many who heard him were astonished, saying, 'Where did this man get all this? What is the wisdom given to him?' " (6:2).

His *works* are an equal source of amazement:

He has power over spirits of evil (1:26, 34, 39; 5:13; 7:30).

He cures sicknesses and infirmities (1:30, Simon's mother-in-law; 1:32-34, healing of many; 1:42, a leper; 2:12, a paralytic; 3:5, man with the withered hand; 3:10, many diseased; 5:29, woman with hemorrhage; 6:5, a few sick people; 6:56, the sick; 7:35, deaf and dumb man; 8:23-25, a blind man).

He raises the dead (5:41-42).

He is Lord of nature (4:39; 6:48-51).

He is a new Moses, giver of new desert bread (6:41-44; 8:6-9).

And his *claims* are another source of challenge:

He forgives sins (2:10) and calls sinners (2:17).

He is the eschatological (last times) bridegroom (2:19), the Lord of the Sabbath (2:28; 3:4), kinsman of all who do God's will (3:35) and the reformer of Jewish traditions (7:1-23).

c) Yet reactions to Jesus *were* (and *would be,* even among Mk's readers) varied. The central question of Mk, chs. 1-8, as I have said, is, "Who then is this . . .?" (4:41).

Many refuse to place any belief in Jesus. These include the authorities—the priests, and the scribes and Pharisees (2:6; 2:16-3:6; 7:5; 8:11). They include, too, his own people and fellow townsmen (3:21; 6:2-4). The scribes even attribute his power to Satan (3:22).

Some of the common people, however, are open to belief and are favorably impressed. These include Jews of Capernaum (1:22, 27-28), the leper (1:40), the paralytic and his friends (2:5), the bystanders (2:12), Levi (2:14), people of the Decapolis, the Greek district of the ten cities (5:20), the woman sick for twelve years (5:28-34), the Syrophoenician woman (7:28), the crowd after the cure of the deaf and dumb man (7:37).

Jesus' closest disciples have an ambivalent stance. They were filled with awe after the stilling of the storm (4:11), overcome with amazement (Peter, James, John) after the cure of Jairus' daughter (5:43); utterly astonished after the second storm miracle (6:51).

Yet Mark also, and clearly, presents the disciples as slow learners. "Do you not understand this parable?" (4:13). ". . . they did not understand about the loaves" (6:52). "Then are you also without understanding?" (7:18). "Do you not yet perceive or understand? Are your hearts hardened? Having eyes do you not see, and having ears do you not hear? . . . Do you not yet understand?" (8:17-18, 21).

d) It is only after all this rapid-action presentation of chs. 1-8, chapters filled with Jesus' works and words, filled with reactions pro and con and ambiguous, that Jesus' chosen disciples (and Mk's readers) arrive at the moment of truth. "And he asked them, 'But who do you say that I am?' Peter answered him, 'You are the Christ' " (8:29). With this profession Peter and the disciples and, hopefully, Mk's readers advance a huge step forward in their answer to the question, "Who then is this?" of 4:41.

A clear indication that Mk has designed the first half of his Gospel to lead to the profession of faith in Jesus as the Christ is evident from the extremely clever use he makes of the passages found in 6:30-7:37 and 8:1-26, passages which immediately precede Peter's profession. These two sections are parallel, in the sense that they contain much similar material and climax, each one, in a healing story (of the deaf man first, of the blind man later). This is the way the sections line up:

6:30-34 Feeding of 5,000 (Jews) ———————————— 8:1-9 Feeding of 4,000 (Gentiles?)
6:45-52 Crossing to Bethsaida ——————————— 8:10 Crossing to Dalmanuth
6:52 Loaves not understood ———— 8:11-13 Against Pharisees
6:53-56 Landing: sick come 8:14-21 Loaves not understood
7:1-23 Against Pharisees ——— 8:22 Crossing to Bethsaida
7:24-30 To Tyre-Sidon: healing
7:31-37 Healing of deaf man ———————————— 8:23-26 Healing of blind man

8:29 Peter's "YOU ARE THE CHRIST"

We should note here, *first* that the material on both sides is very similar. Yet Mk retains it all, presumably for a purpose.

Secondly, each column starts with a desert feeding, once of the Jews, the other, seemingly, of Gentiles. Mk wants both versions.

Thirdly, a great deal is made of the fact that the miracle of the loaves was not understood. ". . . they did not understand about the loaves" (6:52). " 'Why do you discuss the fact that you have no bread? Do you not yet perceive or understand? Are your hearts hardened? Having eyes do you not see, and having ears do you not hear? And do you not remember? When I broke the five loaves for the 5,000, how many baskets full of broken pieces did you take up?' They said to him, 'Twelve.' And the seven for the 4,000, how many baskets full of broken pieces did you take up?' And they said to him, 'Seven.' And he said to them, 'Do you not yet understand?' " (8:17-21). The poor reader of Mk must feel like the uncomprehending disciples themselves by this time. Understand *what* about the loaves? The mystery is clarified if one knows that the miraculous feeding of the Exodus story (Ex 16) was expected to be repeated during the messianic age. II Baruch, a first century apocalyptic writing, states this very clearly. When "the Messiah will begin to be revealed . . . the members of the kingdom will be fed with manna from on high for they have come to the consummation of time" (29:7-8). The feedings, consequently, reveal Jesus as the Messiah, as the Christ.

Fourthly, the first sequence ends with the deaf man hearing, the second with the blind man seeing.

It is only after having portrayed Jesus as the giver of Messianic food (twice) and as the healer of the deaf and the blind, and after emphasizing the apostles' blindness and deafness, that Mk spells out Peter's confession. The Markan rhythm and purpose seem clear. The apostles, hitherto blind and deaf, finally recognize in the giver of the Messianic food the Messiah himself. The parallel sequences lead directly to this. And Mk is certainly thinking, too, and with equal insistence, of his own Christian community which recognizes its Messiah in the eucharistic bread received by those (both Jew and Gentile) to whom baptism has given both sight and hearing.

e) From this mid-point of his Gospel Mk is especially intent on two things: he begins to move the story in the direction of Jerusalem (note the geographical references in 8:27; 9:30; 10:32) and Calvary; he insists on a clarification of Jesus as Christ. *What kind of Christ* is Jesus of Nazareth? The word *Christ,* so natural and acceptable to us, had dangerous and misleading implications at the time of Jesus himself. To the Jews of that time "the Christ-the anointed one" meant savior, king, ruler, deliverer—all terms which were at least as false as true when applied to Jesus. For this reason Jesus' Christness had to be illuminated and clarified by his *Son of Man personality and function.* Jesus will be a Son-of-Man Christ.

f) Mk's Son of Man terminology forms a striking synthesis of two Old Testament figures. The phrase itself, Son of Man, echoes Daniel 7 in which the Son of Man appears in an eschatological judgment scene. And this is part of Mk's presentation and description of Jesus. The other image is that of Isaiah's Suffering Servant (cf. especially Is. 52:13-53:12) *who is delivered up and lays down his life for the sins of the many.* It seems to me that every occurrence of "Son of Man" in Mk refers to one or other of these two Old Testament figures. Thus:

Isaiah's Servant	*Daniel's Son of Man*
2:10 ". . . The Son of Man has power on earth to forgive sins."	8:38 ". . . of him will the Son of Man also be ashamed when he comes in the glory of his Father with the holy angels."
9:9 ". . . to tell no one what they had seen until the Son of Man should have risen from the dead." (cf. Is 52:13)	13:26 "And then they will see the Son of Man coming in clouds with great power and glory."
9:12 "how is it written of the Son of Man that he should suffer many things . . ."	14:62 ". . . and you will see the Son of Man sitting at the right hand of Power and coming with the clouds of heaven."
9:31 "The Son of Man will be delivered into the hands of men, and they will kill him; and when he is killed, after three days he will rise."	
10:33-34 ". . . the Son of Man will be delivered to the chief priests and the scribes; and they will condemn him to the Gentiles; and they will mock him and spit upon him, and scourge him, and kill him; and after three days he will rise."	
10:45 "For the Son of Man also came not to be served but to serve, and to give his life as a ransom for many."	
14:21 "For the Son of Man goes as it is written of him, but woe to that man by whom the Son of Man is betrayed."	
14:41 ". . . the Son of Man is betrayed into the hands of sinners."	

The only instance of "Son of Man" which does not obviously fit into these two categories is that of 2:28: ". . . so the Son of Man is Lord even of the Sabbath."

Probably, however, this refers to Dn 7:14 where the Son of Man is given complete dominion. With the exception of 2:10, all the "Servant" Son of Man usages occur after the middle of ch. 8, the Gospel's watershed.

g) What this means is that Jesus is, indeed, Christ, but on his own and his Father's terms. He is Christ mainly as suffering servant. Listen to Isaiah's description. "He was despised and rejected by men, a man of sorrows . . . Surely he had borne our griefs and carried our sorrows. He was wounded for our transgressions, he was bruised for our iniquities; upon him was the chastisement that made us whole, and with his stripes we are healed. All we like sheep have gone astray; we have turned everyone to his own way; and the Lord has laid on him the iniquity of us all. He was oppressed and he was afflicted, yet he opened not his mouth; like a lamb that is led to the slaughter, and like a sheep that before its shearers is dumb, so he opened not his mouth . . . he was cut off out of the land of the living, stricken for the transgression of my people . . . when he makes himself an offering for sin, he shall see his offspring, he shall prolong his days . . . by his knowledge shall the righteous one, my servant, make many to be accounted righteous; and he shall bear their iniquities . . . because he poured out his soul to death and was numbered with the transgressors; yet he bore the sin of many and made intercession for the transgressors" (Is 53:3-12).

h) Two words of extreme importance in the Greek text of Is 53 are *paradidonai* = to hand over (v. 6 and twice in v. 12) and *hamartia* = sin (vv. 4,5,6,10,12). The servant's life is handed over, or delivered, but not to useless destruction. It is delivered as a saving offering for the sins of the many. The same verb, *paradidonai,* is used continuously by Mk in his references to the passion (9:31; 10:33; 14:10,11,18,21,41,42,44; 15:1,10,15). Jesus is Christ, but a Christ who as suffering servant will lay down his life for the sins of mankind.

i) It is because Jesus is a suffering-servant-Christ that the "Messianic secret" is part of Mk's presentation. What is meant by this is that, ordinarily, those who recognize Jesus as Christ, or who are in position to do so, are commanded to keep their partial knowledge secret (1:25, 34, 43-44; 3:12; 5:43; 7:36; 8:26, 30; 9:9). With this technique Mk stresses the important truth that only those can truly know and confess Jesus as Christ who can see and accept him in his servant role. Such a confession was possible only after the crucifixion, the moment of supreme servanthood.

j) It is extremely important, and the key to the whole of Mk's Gospel, to note how he broadens this servant theology of the Christ to embrace Jesus' disciples also. The second part of the Gospel (8:30ff.) contains in successive chapters three parallel references to Jesus' passion. Each has the same basic structure of prediction, misunderstanding, and teaching. Let's look at these for a moment.

Prediction	Misunderstanding	Teaching
1) Mk 8:30ff.		
And he began to teach them that the Son of Man must suffer many things, and be rejected by the elders and the chief priests and the scribes, and be killed, and after three days rise again.	And Peter took him and began to rebuke him. But turning and seeing his disciples, he rebuked Peter and said, "Get behind me, Satan! For you are not on the side of God, but of men."	And he called to him the multitude with his disciples, and said to them, "If any man come after me, let him deny himself and take up his cross and follow me. For whoever would save his life will lose it; and whoever loses his life for my sake and the gospel's will save it."
2) Mk 9:31ff.		
. . . for he was teaching his disciples, saying to them, "The Son of man will be delivered into the hands of men, and they will kill him; and when he is killed after three days he will rise."	. . . and when he was in the house he asked them, "What were you discussing on the way?" But they were silent; for on the way they were discussing who was the greatest.	. . . and he said to them, "If any one would be first, he must be last of all and servant of all."
3) Mk 10:33ff.		
". . . the Son of man will be delivered to the chief priests and the scribes and they will condemn him to death, and deliver him to the Gentiles; and they will mock him, and spit upon him, and scourge him, and kill him; and after three days he will rise.	And James and John . . . said to him, "Grant us to sit, one at your right hand and one at your left, in your glory. But Jesus said to them, "You do not know what you are asking. Are you able to drink the cup that I drink, or be baptized with the baptism with which I am baptized?" And they said to him, "We are able." And Jesus said to them, "The cup that I drink you	And Jesus . . . said, "You know that those who are supposed to rule over the Gentiles lord it over them, and their great men exercise authority over them. But it shall not be so among you; but whoever would be great among you must be slave of all. For the Son of man also came not to be served but to serve, and to give his life as a ransom for many."

will drink; and with the
baptism with which I am
baptized, you will be
baptized; but to sit at my
right hand or at my left
is not mine to grant, but
it is for those for whom
it has been prepared.''

What we have just read in these three parallel passages is a truly extraordinary combination of both deep theology and an experienced realization of human weakness. In all three *predictions,* with the third being the most explicit, Jesus tells of his coming death of suffering, to be followed by resurrection. The servant Son of man will indeed ''be exalted and lifted up'' (Is 52:13), but first he must be ''like a lamb . . . led to the slaughter,'' ''cut off out of the land of the living,'' the one who has ''poured out his soul to death . . . numbered among the transgressors'' as ''he bore the sin of many'' (Is 53:7,8,12).

In all three negative reactions the disciples—forerunners of Christians down to our own times—greeted with less than enthusiastic welcome this reality of the suffering Jesus. Peter rebukes Jesus in ch. 8; the disciples turn to discussing who is the greatest in ch. 9; James and John prefer to think about the glory seats in ch. 10. A suffering-servant Christ was, and still is, hard theology to swallow.

And things get worse before they get better. Jesus proceeds in the three *teachings* to extend his cross to the disciples. They, too, must take up the cross (ch. 8), become servants of all (ch. 9), become the servants and the slaves of all (ch. 10). Only thus, and only then, can they be followers of that Son of man who ''came not to be served but to serve, and to give his life as a ransom for many'' (10:45). Servant Christ demands servant Christians.

If we add to the parallels presented above the fact that these predictions and teachings are all connected with geographical indications (Caesarea Philippi in 8:31, through Galilee in 9:30, ''And they were on the way, going up to Jerusalem'' in 10:32) it is hard not to conclude that Mk is presenting a Way to the Cross scheme, a Way to the Cross that must be shared by both Jesus and by all who claim to be his disciples. Is this not the purpose of the subsequent account of blind Bartimaeus who, once faith had given him sight, left all—even his tossed off mantle—''and followed him on the way'' (10:52)? On the way? What way? Mk has already told us in v. 22, ''on the way, going up to Jerusalem'' as he also tells us in 11:1, the first verse after the Bartimaeus story, ''And when they drew near to Jerusalem . . .'' As we confess Jesus as Lord we receive our faith-sight and, like Bartimaeus, are called to follow Jesus to Jerusalem, the site of servant crucifixion.

Another way that Mk has of presenting the same theology of the cross is the parallel he sets up between Jesus and both the Baptist and the disciples. John the Baptist preached (1:7) and was delivered up (1:14); Jesus preached (1:14) and was delivered up (9:31; 10:33); Christians, too, are called to preach (1:1; 13:10) and will be delivered up (13:9-13). Indeed their tribulations are painted in almost the same hues as those of Jesus himself (13:9). The followers of Jesus are being invited by Mk's Gospel to be suffering servants as was their Lord before them. If it is true that Mk is writing to the Church of his own time, it becomes obvious that Mk's Church is a martyr Church to which the evangelist offers not solace but example and certain hope. This helps to illumine for us the seemingly strange passage in 10:38-39 which speaks of James and John drinking the cup which Jesus drinks and being baptized with the baptism in which he is baptized. The cup and baptism refer, certainly, to Jesus' sufferings—sufferings which he will drink and into which he will be plunged. But it is impossible for Mk's Christian readers not to think at the same time of their own cup, the Eucharist, and their own initial ceremony which baptized them into Christ. Mk's full thought, consequently, is that both baptism and the Eucharist relate the Christian to their suffering-servant Lord. (This teaching is even clearer in Paul's theology of baptism in Rom 6:3 and of the Eucharist in 1 Cor 11:26.)

k) Another truly extraordinary bit of Markan theology appears in the use he makes of the other title of Jesus which appears in 1:1, "Son of God." It, or its equivalent, can be found in the Gospel seven times, five before the passion narrative. It appears in the opening verse (though there is some textual difficulty concerning this as it is missing in some manuscripts), is used twice by unclean spirits over whom Jesus exercises his authority, but who are presumed to have supernatural powers (3:11; 5:7), and twice again by the heavenly Father (1:11; 9:7). Jesus consents to the title as used by the high priest early in the passion narrative (14:61-62). But the climactic and most profound profession of faith in the Gospel is uttered by a Gentile, a Roman soldier, who recognizes Jesus as Son of God precisely at the culmination of his sacrifice, at the moment of his death on the cross. Mark has framed both the *Christ* and *Son of God* titles within the borders of servanthood and suffering. And for his Christian readers he has also bound his presentation of the good news with front and back covers both bearing the same title, "Jesus, Son of God" (1:1; 15:39).

l) There is one final faith statement before Mk brings his version of the good news to its conclusion: "Do not be amazed; you seek Jesus of Nazareth, who was crucified. *He has risen, he is not here;* see the place where they laid him" (16:6). And this is, indeed, the good news of the Lord. Jesus, who both as Christ and Son of God, was destined for salvific suffering and death was also destined for exaltation and glory. "Behold my servant shall prosper," says Is 52:13, *"he shall be exalted and lifted up, and shall be very high."* Jesus passes through cross to glory. And so, too, Mk assures his readers, will those who take up his cross and follow him (8:34-35; 13:13, 26-27).

m) Mark's Eschatology, his Doctrine of the Last Days and of Christ's Second Coming

To us modern readers, a belief in the end of this world and of Christ's second coming has little urgency. There is, to be sure, the modern threat of atomic warfare and the horrifying realization that the simple push of not too many buttons could wipe out a large part of world culture and population. But the tying together of a divinely programmed consummation of the world and Christ's return is hardly part of a Christian's faith-dynamism. It is, consequently, difficult to realize just how much an influence that belief had on the Christians of the first century. In Mk's Gospel the belief is strong, and the texts that indicate it are multiple and clear. Take the following two as instances:

"For whoever is ashamed of me and of my words in this adulterous and sinful generation, of him will the Son of man also be ashamed, when he comes in the glory of his Father with the holy angels. And he said to them, 'Truly, I say to you, there are some standing here who will not taste death before they see the kingdom of God come with power' " (8:38-9:1).

"And Jesus said, 'I am; and you will see the Son of man sitting at the right hand of power, and coming with the clouds of heaven' " (14:62).

Moreover, the whole of ch. 13 is a statement of belief in an approaching world-end, with an accompanying persecution of Christians and a rewarding return of the Lord. Thus:

"And when you hear of wars and rumors of wars, do not be alarmed; this must take place, but the end is not yet. For nation will rise against nation, and kingdom against kingdom; there will be earthquakes in various places, there will be famines; this is but the beginning of the sufferings. But take heed to yourselves; for they will deliver you up to councils; and you will be beaten in synagogues; and you will stand before governors and kings for my sake, to bear testimony before them. And the gospel must first be preached to all nations. And when they bring you to trial and deliver you up, do not be anxious beforehand what you are to say; but say whatever is given you in that hour, for it is not you who speak, but the Holy Spirit. And brother will deliver up brother to death, and the father his child, and children will rise against parents and have them put to death; and you will be hated by all for my name's sake. But he who endures to the end will be saved" (vv. 7-13).

"For in those days there will be such tribulation as has not been from the beginning of the creation which God created until now, and never will be. And if the Lord had not shortened the days, no human being would be saved; but for the sake of the elect, whom he chose, he shortened the days" (vv. 19-20).

"But in those days, after that tribulation, the sun will be darkened, and the moon will not give its light, and the stars will be falling from heaven, and the powers in the heavens will be shaken. And then they will see the Son of man coming in clouds with great power and glory. And then he will send out the angels, and gather his elect from the four winds, from the ends of the earth to the ends of heaven. From the fig tree learn its lesson: as soon as its branch becomes tender and puts forth its leaves, you know that summer is near. So also, when you see these things taking place, you know that he is near, at the very gates. Truly, I say to you, this generation will not pass away before all these things take place" (vv. 24-30).

Yet the hour is uncertain, no one knows it, "not even the angels in heaven, nor the Son, but only the Father" (v. 32). So the important warning for Mk's community and for his readers is, "Take heed . . . watch!"

This assurance of a shattering world-end in the near future was, for Mk and community, only partially realized. For them one world would come to an end when, in 70 A.D., Jerusalem and its temple would lie destroyed and, with that, Jewish sacrifice and priesthood would cease. That Mk has some realization of this seems certain from the way he joins the rending of the temple veil to the moment of Jesus' death: "And Jesus uttered a loud cry and breathed his last. And the curtain of the temple was torn in two, from top to bottom" (15:37-38). Yet Christ's return would not accompany this disaster, nor would the world change configuration. I suspect—indeed it is hard to doubt—that Mk would be amazed if, given a vision of our twentieth century world, he had found the expected return of Jesus still not accomplished. But he might also be amazed, and intensely satisfied, that his central teaching of Jesus as Man-for-Others, his portrayal of the Lord as suffering-servant who summons his followers to a servant role, has emerged with a force and urgency and appeal perhaps unmatched in any preceding century.

3. Author

The Gospel itself leaves its author anonymous. There is no statement within it telling us who the author is, nor do we know whether or not the original title—if there was any—included Mark's name. What we do know is that Church tradition as far back as early in the second century has always attributed this Gospel to *Mark*. About 130 A.D. a Christian named Papias who lived in Hierapolis, not far from Ephesus in Asia Minor, stated that Mark, the interpreter of Peter, wrote down what he remembered of the Lord's words and deeds. This extremely early tradition seems very credible, especially since it is hard to imagine why, if the Gospel's author was unknown, it would have been assigned to a very secondary or unknown New Testament figure rather than to one of the apostles themselves.

It is quite possible, though not capable of proof, that this is the Mark referred to in a whole series of New Testament writings. Thus, Acts 12:12 speaks of ". . . the house of Mary, the mother of John whose other name was Mark, where many were gathered together and were praying." Mark, cousin of Barnabas (Col 4:10), was taken by Barnabas and Paul on the first missionary journey but abandoned the venture in its early stages (Acts 13:13), thus laying the ground for a subsequent dissension between Paul and Barnabas (Acts 15:37-38). He is mentioned favorably in later Pauline literature (Philem 24; Col 4:10; 2 Tim 4:11) and in 1 Pet 5:13.

4. Place and Time of Composition

Here, again, we enter into disputed territory. Papias—whom we met above—connects Mk's Gospel to Peter who was, in all probability, martyred in Rome. A passage from 1 Pet links Peter to Mark to Babylon, which latter is probably a cryptic reference to Rome (1 Pet 5:13). Another description of Mk's Gospel in what is perhaps a second century writing (the anti-Marcionite prologue to the Gospel of Mk) also declares that Mk was the interpreter of Peter and that, after Peter's death, he wrote this Gospel in the regions of Italy.

The Church Father, Irenaeus—who actually visited Rome in the latter half of the second century A.D.—also locates the composition of this Gospel in Rome. And the "martyr" spirit of the Christians whom the Gospel addresses certainly fits well into the atmosphere of Rome in the sixties, a time when Nero was persecuting Christians with unrestrained violence, and when both Peter and Paul were martyred in, or just outside of, the city. A Roman origin would also explain the rapid circulation of the Gospel, a circulation that put copies of it in the hands of both Matthew and Luke within one or two decades. It would also help explain how it was that this writing, though soon regarded as little more than an abbreviation of Mt, was accepted into the Christian Canon, the official catalogue of accepted Christian writings.

Yet some scholars remain unconvinced of a Roman birthplace and incline toward an Eastern locale, perhaps Syria, where Mk's community would have been subject to both Jewish and Gentile influences.

So far as dating is concerned, Mk wrote just before or after the destruction of Jerusalem by the Roman legions, therefore about 70 A.D. Scholars argue in both directions from the descriptions which ch. 13 gives us of the destruction of the temple and city of Jerusalem. Some believe that the details so parallel the actual events which took place in 70 A.D. that they must have been written after that date. Others argue to just the opposite conclusion. A round number, about 70 A.D., is the best we can do at the moment.

5. Intended Audience

The evidence we have favors the opinion that Mk's Good News was directed toward a community which included both Jew and Gentile, with a certain careful emphasis given to the Gentiles in the group. It is considerably less Jewish than Matthew's version. Consider, for example, such differences as are apparent in:

G.P. #216, where Mt includes the Jewish concern, ''on the Sabbath''; G.P. #116, where Mt, but not Mk, has Jesus sent ''only to the lost sheep of the house of Israel.''

Mk also adds explanations of Jewish practices, explanations that would be superfluous for Jewish readers. Thus: 7:3-4, an explanation of eating bread with defiled hands; 14:12, an explanation that Passover lambs were slaughtered on the first day of Unleavened Bread; 15:42, stating that Preparation Day was the day before the Sabbath. Mk also translates Aramaic words: 3:17, Boanerges means *Sons of Thunder;* 5:41, Talitha cumi means *Child, get up;* 7:11, Corban signifies *set apart* while in 7:34, Ephphatha means *Be opened;* in 10:46, Bartimaeus is translated *Son of Timaeus;* in 14:36, Abba means *Father;* in 15:22, Golgotha is translated *skull;* and in 15:34, Eloi, Eloi, lama sabachtani means *My God, my God, why hast thou forsaken me?''*

The Church which Mk has most directly in view, all agree, is a martyr Church, a persecuted Church. It is a Church were a Christian may well be called upon to ''deny himself and take up his cross and follow'' Christ (8:34). It is a Church where Christians are asked to drink the cup which Jesus drank, and be baptized with the baptism in which he was baptized (10:39). It is a Church whose members are delivered up, beaten in synagogues, and where testimony before kings and governors may be required (13:9). It is, finally, a Church where brothers, parents, children may be handed over to death by their own families (13:12). This makes of Mk's Gospel an austere document shaped by the ordeals of the period of its composition. For those who place its origin in Rome, the situation is clear and self-explanatory. Mk's Gospel is addressed to the martyr Church of Rome, reeling under the persecution unleashed by Nero and severely shocked and shaken by the recent slayings of both Peter and Paul. For others, the view is less sharply focused. Mk addresses a Christian Church, immediately before or after the fall of Jerusalem, suffering persecution from the Romans for being Jewish, and from the Jews for being Christian. According to both opinions, Mk proposes, as exemplar, the servant Christ whose divine sonship was recognized as he hung on the cross, and, as final reward, the coming of the servant Son of man in glory. And just as, at the end of the Gospel story, the disciples await the reappearance of the resurrected Lord, so must Mk's readers await the reappearance in glory of Jesus at his expected return.

6. Resumé

a) Title: The Good News of Jesus, *Christ, Son of God.* This points ahead to the great professions of belief: Peter's "You are the Christ" in 8:29 and the centurion's "Truly this man was Son of God" in 15:39.

b) Chapters leading to Peter's confession (8:29).

c) This initial profession of faith is followed immediately by the introduction of the servant theme which occurs so frequently thereafter. Jesus is truly the Christ, the Messiah, of 8:29—his rebuke of Peter does not follow immediately after Peter's confession and is not directed at it—but that Messiah is the suffering servant of Yahweh who must suffer and lay down his life for the sins of others. This will lead to his ultimate glorification as in Is 52:13 and 53:12a. The theme points, therefore, to both the cross and the empty tomb.

d) The centurion's confession in 15:39 is a true profession of belief in the sense that it is the conclusion to which the reader should arrive when presented with the words and works and life-story of Jesus. And this is Mk's precise intent—to lead the reader to the point where he or she can either make a profession of faith in Jesus, or strengthen such a profession already made.

e) Intermingled with the theme of the Servant is that of Daniel's Son of Man coming in judgment (Dn 7). This, too, occurs only in the second half of the Gospel. It projects the life of the Servant (and the thought of the reader) past the passion and glorification to the future coming of Christ, to what Paul terms the *parousia*.

7. A Few Final Thoughts

a) It is interesting and important to note that Peter's words to Cornelius in Acts 10:36-43 are Mark's Gospel in miniature. Read them slowly and see if the basic presentation of Mk does not come to mind. Peter says: "You know the word which he (God) sent to Israel, preaching good news of peace by Jesus Christ (he is Lord of all), the word which was proclaimed throughout all Judea, beginning from Galilee after the baptism which John preached: how God anointed Jesus of Nazareth with the Holy Spirit and with power; how he went about doing good and healing all that were oppressed by the devil, for God was with him. And we are witnesses to all that he did both in the country of the Jews and in Jerusalem. They put him to death by hanging him on a tree; but God raised him on the third day and made him manifest; not to all the people but to us who were chosen by God as witnesses, who ate and drank with him after he rose from the dead. And he commanded us to preach to the people, and to testify that he is the one ordained by God to be judge of the living and the dead. To him all the prophets bear witness that every one who believes in him receives forgiveness of sins through his name.''

It is remarkable how well these eight verses of Acts recapitulate the basic geography and theology of Mark. In both, the geography moves from the baptism of John up to Galilee where Jesus' ministry occurs, and down to Jerusalem where he dies and rises. And, in both, the basic theology centers on the forgiveness of sins (the Servant theme) and on Jesus as judge of the living and the dead (the Son of Man theme). The author of Acts indicates that this is the "good news of peace" (v. 36). It is reasonable to conclude that the essential elements of Mk's presentation resemble the early kerygma, the basic preaching of the primitive Church.

b) Our Christian word "Gospel, good news" is the translation of the Greek, *euangelion* and comes to us from Is 52:7-10. This reads: "How beautiful upon the mountains are the feet of him who brings *good tidings,* who publishes peace, who brings *good tidings* of good, who publishes salvation, who says to Zion, 'Your God reigns.' Hark, your watchmen lift up their voice, together they sing for joy; for eye to eye they see the return of the Lord to Zion. Break forth together into singing, you waste places of Jerusalem; for the Lord has comforted his people, he has redeemed Jerusalem. The Lord has bared his holy arm before the eyes of all the nations; and all the ends of the earth shall see the salvation of our God." By striking coincidence—or is it?—what follows in Isaiah after his "good news" passage is the Fourth Servant Song of 52:13-53:12 which we have already referred to so often. And, indeed, the theology of the suffering servant, of his death for the forgiveness of sin, of his future exaltation and glorification, is the good news which Mark presents with clarity and challenge to us, his readers.

Chapter Six

The Good News According to Matthew

Matthew's version of the good news is, I believe, a revision, a new edition of the Gospel of Mk which Mt has in his possession. This means that Mt is not completely satisfied with Mk's version as sufficient to answer the needs of his community. It also means that Mt possesses information which he can use to revise Mk, material from our proposed Q, a grouping of Jesus' sayings which Lk also possesses, plus material which Mt alone utilizes (M). Mt, then, is Mk plus Q plus M, ordered and shaped by Mt's editorial handicraft. His ultimate thesis—one which controls so much of the Gospel— is stated in his conclusion (28:18-20). Jesus, to whom has been given all authority, transmits this to his chosen apostles, commissioning them to evangelize the world. Matthew's Old Testament model here is Daniel's Son of Man to whom was given "dominion and glory and kingdom, that all peoples, nations, and languages should serve him" (Dn 7:14).

1. Major Divisions

Recent scholarly literature has discussed in great detail possible divisions of Mt's Gospel. As the dust of their labor settles, it seems to me that the best founded division is still that which held the field before the recent debate began. This division is based on a key phrase that Mt repeats at the end of Jesus' five sermons. The literal translation is: *"And it happened when Jesus finished . . .,"* six words in the original Greek as in this English version. These six words, always in identical order in the Greek original, are found at 7:28; 11:1; 13:53; 19:1; 26:1. Each phrase puts an end to a teaching section in Mt.

Taking these sections all together we find five booklets of Jesus' teaching, or five booklets of Christian *Torah,* of Christian revelation. There are solid grounds for believing that Mt has organized his Gospel in such a fashion that it can be seen to take precedence over the five books of Jewish *Torah,* Moses' Pentateuch, the first five books of the Bible. Each sermon in Mt is preceded by a narrative that appears to prepare for the sermon. And the first two and last three chapters are separated from the sermon sections to constitute a formal beginning and ending. That gives us the following major divisions:

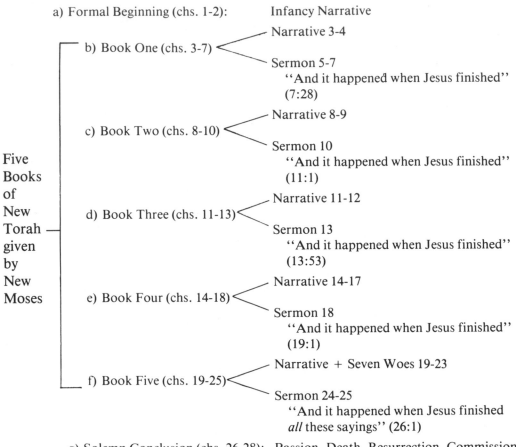

a) Formal Beginning (chs. 1-2): Infancy Narrative

Five Books of New Torah given by New Moses

b) Book One (chs. 3-7)
— Narrative 3-4
— Sermon 5-7
  "And it happened when Jesus finished" (7:28)

c) Book Two (chs. 8-10)
— Narrative 8-9
— Sermon 10
  "And it happened when Jesus finished" (11:1)

d) Book Three (chs. 11-13)
— Narrative 11-12
— Sermon 13
  "And it happened when Jesus finished" (13:53)

e) Book Four (chs. 14-18)
— Narrative 14-17
— Sermon 18
  "And it happened when Jesus finished" (19:1)

f) Book Five (chs. 19-25)
— Narrative + Seven Woes 19-23
— Sermon 24-25
  "And it happened when Jesus finished *all* these sayings" (26:1)

g) Solemn Conclusion (chs. 26-28): Passion, Death, Resurrection, Commission

This leaves us with five books of teaching, and with an overall division into seven parts. Now Mt likes groups of seven. His genealogy (1:1-17) is based on fourteen, a multiple of seven; his version of the Our Father has seven petitions (6:5-13); there are seven loaves in 15:34, seven brothers in 22:25, seven woes in 23:13-36, and we are asked to forgive, not seven times, but till seventy times seven (18:22). The division proposed, therefore, is based on Mt's own literary clues—the closing phrase of all the sermons— and on his proclivity for the number seven. The division also happens to be easy to memorize. If you know that Mt begins with two chapters of infancy narratives, and that the sermons occur in chs. 5-7,10,13,18, 24-25, everything else fits into place. This rigorously organized division presents Matthew to us as a planning expert, a man strongly inclined to have a place for everything and everything in its place. He would have kept an immaculate kitchen.

2. Mt's Theology and Procedure

a) MT'S FORMAL BEGINNING (chs. 1-2) emphasizes theology, the God-meaning he sees in Jesus. Thus Jesus is *"Christ,* the son of *David,* the son of *Abraham"* (1:1). With this triple phrasing Mt sinks Christian roots deeply into Jewish soil. The historical Jesus of Nazareth is the Jewish Messiah-*Christ,* a descendant of *David,* Jewish king par excellence, to whom was given the promise of an everlasting kingdom (2 Sam 7); and a descendant of *Abraham,* father of the Jewish people (Gen 12:2; 17:4-8).

Jesus, child of the Old Testament, is also a new creation, and this by God's action. This is the theology of the virgin birth (2:18-25). God initiates a new era.

Jesus as Messiah is a new David. Mt signals this with a triple flashing of his "fourteen" spotlight. "So all the generations from Abraham to David were fourteen generations, and from David to the deportation to Babylon fourteen generations, and from the deportation to Babylon to the Christ fourteen generations" (1:17). The numerical equivalent of David's name in Hebrew (D = 4 + V = 6 + D = 4) totals 14.

The Magi story (2:1-12) is a theology of universalism. Jesus, rejected by a troubled king and a troubled city of Jerusalem (2:3), is sought out and worshipped by Gentiles.

The most influential theology underlying these two chapters, however, is one that builds up a detailed parallel between Jesus and the Old Testament exodus events in which Moses and the people Israel participated. Note the striking similarities:

Old Israel and Moses	*Jesus as New Israel and New Moses*
To Egypt under Joseph	To Egypt under Joseph (2:13)
Sojourn in Egypt	Sojourn in Egypt (2:14)
Slaughter of male children by Pharaoh	Slaughter of male children by Herod (2:16)
Moses saved	Jesus saved (2:13-15)
Exodus under Moses	Christian Exodus with Jesus (2:20-23)
Water (Ex 14)	Water (3:13)
Sonship (Ex 4:22)	Sonship (3:17)
Desert (Ex 15ff.)	Desert (4:1)
Temptations (Ex 16-17)	Temptations (4:1-11)
Moses fasts forty days (Ex 24:18; 34:28)	Jesus fasts forty days (4:2)
Mt. Sinai (Ex 24:16-17)	Mount of Beatitudes (5:1ff.)
Ten plague miracles (Ex 7-12)	Ten Christ miracles (cc. 8-9)

This presentation of Jesus as both the new Israel and the new Moses is so dominating in Mt's mind that he borrows, as the divine signal for Joseph, Mary, and child to return from Egypt, words previously used in the book of Exodus to describe a return of Moses.

"Go back . . . for all the men who were seeking your life are dead" (Ex 4:19).

"Go . . . for all those who sought the child's life are dead" (Mt 2:20).

This initial Jesus-Moses parallel is already a long step toward the comparison which Mt will make between the new and old Moses in the Sermon on the Mount.

One final Matthean interest reveals itself. Mt refers to prophetic fulfillments in

1:23, "Behold a virgin . . ."; in 2:6, "And you, O Bethlehem . . ."; in 2:17, "A voice was heard in Ramah . . ."; in 2:23, "He shall be called a Nazarene." Mt clearly wants to present Jesus as the fulfillment to the Old Testament prophetic revelations. In doing this it is also clear that he has strong Jewish interests.

b) BOOK ONE (chs. 3-7), IDEALS OF THE KINGDOM

Narrative (chs. 3-4). Mt, throughout his Gospel, uses narrative sections to prepare for the sermons. At this point, though following the basic Markan order, he is moving toward the first discourse, the Sermon on the Mount. In preparation, he treats of:

—John the Baptist (3:1-12) who appears as a new Elijah to fulfill the expectation for the return of "Elijah the prophet, before the great and terrible day of the Lord comes" (Mal 4:5). John's garments are patterned after those of Elijah (2 Kg 1:8).

—Jesus' baptism (3:13-17), in which he is presented as God's beloved son in whom the Father is well pleased. The second half of that statement is from Is 42:1, the first of the Suffering Servant songs which so impressed Mark.

—The temptations (4:1-11), which Jesus overcomes in contrast to the old Israel which succumbed to temptation in the desert. Besides this new Israel-old Israel comparison, Mt is also interested in negating a false type of Messianism, one based on material things, spectacular performance, and power. A look at G.P. #8 at this point indicates how Mt and Lk—or their common source—have built up the much simpler presentation of Mk. Even so, Mt concludes with Mk's final phrasing.

Following in rapid fashion come the initial proclamation of the kingdom (4:17), the call of the first disciples (4:18-22), the gathering together and healing of the sick, the demoniacs, the epileptics, and the paralytics. These cures bring to Jesus large numbers of people, the crowds which provide the audience for the discourse (5:1; 7:28).

First Discourse: Sermon on the Mount (chs. 5-7)

This first sermon is a Christian manifesto, a presentation of Christian outlook and Christian practice. A brief look at the G.P. Index, #18-44, will show us that almost all of Mt's material here is shared by Lk (column 6). And it is interesting to note how much can be found in Lk's chapter six, his sermon on the plain. Even more, Lk's chapter six material is essentially in the same order as the parallels in Mt. Thus column six, paralleling Mt's order, lists Lk 6:12, 20, 20-23, 29-30, 27-28, 32-36, 37-38, 41-42, 31, 43-45, 46, 47-49. This gives ground for suspecting that this sermon had been put into shape before Mt and Lk wrote their gospels. And it may have been quite independent of Q. To this primitive sermon Mt, as will be his custom throughout the Gospel, has added a large amount of other material. Some scholars have found the sermon's thematic statement in 5:20—"For I tell you, unless your righteousness exceeds that of the *scribes* and *Pharisees,* you will never enter the kingdom of God." If this be true, the sermon would divide itself into an introduction, a section regarding the scribes, another referring to the Pharisees, and a final part dealing directly with the righteousness expected of Jesus' disciples. This gives the following outline:

Introduction 5:2-16

> The Beatitudes (vv. 2-12)
> Disciples as salt and light of world (13-16)

Law 5:17-48 (directed against scribes, the lawyers, and theologians of the day)

> Greater perfection of Christian Torah as against Mosaic Torah
> "You shall not kill . . . But I say to you" (21-24)
> "You shall not commit adultery . . . But I say" (27-28)
> "Whoever divorces his wife . . . But I say" (31-32)
> "You shall not swear falsely . . . But I say" (33-37)
> "An eye for an eye . . . But I say" (38-42)
> ". . . love your neighbor and hate your enemy. But I say" (43-48).

Worship 6:1-18 (against popular piety of Pharisees)

> Almsgiving (2-4)
> Prayer (5-15)
> Fasting (16-18)
> In all three references a strong contrast is drawn between sincere internal worship and that performed in public to capture attention and praise.

Righteousness of Jesus' Disciples 6:19-7:27

> Trust in providence (6:19-34)
> Kindness (7:1-12) "So whatever you wish that men would do to you, do so to them; for this is the Law and the prophets" (v. 12).
> Conclusion (7:13-27)
> > The Two Ways (13-14)
> > Necessity of *doing* (15-27)

"And when Jesus finished these sayings, the crowds were astonished at his teaching, for he taught them *as one who had authority* and *not as the scribes*" (7:28). With this formula of transition, Mt completes this first book with an insistence on themes close to his heart. Jesus, teaching with authority, is a new Moses, greater than the original. And his teaching is superior to that of the scribes, an allusion probably to the official teaching emanating in the days of Mt's Church from the new Jewish center of Jamnia (Jabneh) to which the whole of Mt's Gospel reacts. We will say more about this later, but it might help at the moment to note that with the destruction of Jerusalem in 70 A.D., a Jewish center of study began to flourish in Jamnia where scholars had fled from Jerusalem. Jerusalem was now destroyed, as was the temple. With the cessation of sacrifices, priests had lost their function. All that was left was "the book," the Jewish scriptures. To them the scholars in Jamnia gave their complete and dedicated attention. Their authority and interpretation must have soon provided a vigorous challenge to Jewish Christians for whom, not Moses and his writings, but Jesus and his teachings were now the supreme guide.

c) BOOK TWO (chs. 8-10), DISCIPLESHIP

Narrative (chs. 8-9)

The first sermon concluded, Mt returns to the Markan sequence of G.P. #45, 52-54 = Mk 1:40-2:22. But Mk's healing of a leper (#45) and of a paralytic (#52) plus the call of Levi (#53) appear to trigger off an idea for Mt, the possibility of a discourse on discipleship. This will occur in Mt, ch. 10, and we can now see him prepare for it in chs. 8-9. In these two chapters Mt will include six references to discipleship: nature of discipleship in #49; power given to men in #52 = Mt 9:8; call of Matthew in #53; fasting on the part of disciples in #54; harvest plentiful but laborers few in #58; summoning of the Twelve (#58).

All of these references are a fine preparation for the sermon. To them Mt has joined another preparatory element, though it may seem less significant at first view. He has accepted the two healing miracles of Mk, i.e., #45, the leper and #52, the paralytic and added to them eight others for a grand total of ten. (Jesus, powerful in WORD, Book One, will now become Jesus powerful in WORK.) Mk's earlier miracles of #13-14 which were absent at that point in Mt appear now in #47-48. Mt has saved them for this spot. Future miracles in Mk #105, #106, #107 are also found at this point in Mt #50, #51, #55. It becomes evident that Mt has intentionally put together a whole collection of miracle stories as preparatory to the sermon of ch. 10. Why? What purpose do they serve? For Mt these works are certain signs that the kingdom of heaven has arrived and with it the time for Christian discipleship. Mt is thinking of Isaian passages which describe such works as *signs of the day of the Lord.* For example:

> Is 35:4-6—"Say to those who are of a fearful heart, Be strong, fear not! Behold, your God will come with vengeance, with the recompense of God. He will come and *save* you (Mt 8:25). Then the eyes of the *blind* shall be opened (Mt 9:27-31), and the ears of the *deaf* unstopped; then shall the *lame* man leap like a hart (Mt 9:7), and the tongue of the *dumb* sing for joy" (Mt 9:32-34).
>
> Is 29:18-19—"In that day the *deaf* shall hear the words of a book, and out of their gloom and darkness the eyes of the *blind* shall see. The *meek* shall obtain fresh joy in the Lord, and the *poor* among men shall exult in the Holy One of Israel.
>
> Is 26:19—"Your *dead* will come to life, their corpses will rise. . ."

Mt has, consequently, used Mk's brief material on disciples and healings, but has adroitly built up the whole complex to lay heavy stress on disciples, discipleship and the miracle signs of the arrival of that kingdom into which the disciples enter. Finally, his references in 9:36-10:4 to the shepherdless sheep, to the harvest and laborers, and to the initial commission of the twelve disciples completes his elegantly organized preparation for the discipleship discourse.

Second Discourse: Discipleship (10:5-42)

In this discourse Mt insists that the authority of Jesus to preach (chs. 5-7) and to act (chs. 8-9) has been transmitted by him to his disciples—and also to their successors in the time of Matthew himself. The chapter gives evidence of both of these historical layers, the period of Jesus and the later time of the evangelist.

Verses 5-15 refer to the time of Jesus himself. His own practice of going to the lost sheep of the house of Israel is instanced in vv. 5-6. Then follows (vv. 7-8) the transmission of authority—a preview of 28:18-20—to preach and to heal. The brief span of the mission makes the radical poverty of vv. 9-10 no less an ideal but, perhaps, a bit more understandable. The disciples, on the other hand, deserve the aid of those whom they help. Their preaching will be good news, deserving of acceptance (vv. 14-15).

What follows from v. 16 on seems directed more toward the time of the post-resurrection Church and probably indicates the conditions of Mt's own life time. The disciples' fate will entail suffering as did that of their master: they will be hailed before legal and religious authorities, before councils, synagogues, governors and kings (shades of Paul of Tarsus!). Families—and especially Jewish families—will split over the acceptance or rejection of Jesus as the Christ. The picture is one of Roman and Jewish opposition: the circumstances fit well into the period after 70 A.D.

Verses 26-33 are meant to be an encouragement with their triple "Fear not" of vv. 26, 28, 31. In similar fashion God had instructed the prophet Jeremiah (Jer 1:8). And, indeed, Mt speaks also of the sufferings which prophets have had in the past and will sustain in the future (5:12; 23:34). They are now being endured by the Christian prophets of Mt's era.

Verses 34-39 are a second spelling out of the difficulties that await the Christian disciple, deep conflicts even within one's own family. All this may well be part of the cross which every disciple is asked to shoulder.

The sermon ends with a consoling promise. Those who do accept the disciples accept Christ in them. Great will be the reward of those who accept the invitation which Jesus offers through his own Christian prophets.

Mt's words of transition follow immediately: "And it happened when Jesus finished . . ." (11:1)

d) BOOK THREE (chs. 11-13), KINGDOM IN MYSTERY

Narrative (chs. 11-12)

A look at Mt 11:2-12 in G.P. #64-71 plus #85-89 shows that he is following the general sequence of Mk 2:23-3:35, but with the addition of one non-Markan block, mainly Q, which constitutes ch. 11. This chapter, the result of Mt's personal creativity, helps to illuminate the total purpose of chs. 11-12. Who is this man (the basic question of Mk, chs. 1-8) and who are those who believe in him? The answer will be: Jesus is the WISDOM of God, hidden from the proud, but revealed to the little ones. There is a mystery about Jesus and about his kingdom, just as the kingdom parables of ch. 13 are also dressed in mystery.

The disciples of the Baptist ask, "Are you he who is to come, or shall we look for another?" (11:3). Jesus responds with an enumeration of the miracles which fulfill Is 35:4-6; 29:18-19; 26:9. The blind, lame, lepers, deaf, dead, and the poor have all been graced by his saving presence (11:5).

The crowds are perplexed, critical of a man who eats and drinks, and who is a friend of tax collectors and sinners (11:16-19).

The towns in which he has worked miracles (Chorazin, Bethsaida, Capernaum) refuse to believe (11:20-24).

Who have believed? The little ones who have accepted the Son's unique revelation of the Father (11:25-27). It is this Son, gentle and lowly in heart, who is the WISDOM of God. This description of Jesus as wisdom is presented clearly in both #67 and 68. Paragraph 67 (Mt 11:25-27) reads strikingly like something out of the Gospel of John. Jesus has come as revealer of the Father, as the Word which God speaks to reveal himself to believers. Jesus is God's self-expression, the mirror of the Father, God's wisdom incarnate. Paragraph 68, on the other hand, is patterned after many passages of the Old Testament wisdom literature. This deliberate patterning would tell any reader sensitive to Old Testament terminology that Mt wishes to present Jesus in the robes of divine wisdom. Note the similarity between what is said of Jesus in #68, Mt 11:28-30, and the description of wisdom in the following Old Testament passages:

Proverbs 9:4-5—"Whoever is simple, let him turn in here!
   To him who is without sense she says,
   Come, eat of my bread and drink of the wine I have mixed."
Sirach 24:19-20—"Come to me, you who desire me,
   and eat your fill of my produce.
   For the remembrance of me is sweeter than honey,
   and my inheritance sweeter than the honeycomb.
Sirach 51:23, 26-27—"Draw near to me, you who are untaught,
   and lodge in my school . . .
   Put your neck under the yoke, and let your souls receive instruction;
   it is to be found close by.
   See with your eyes that I have labored little
   and found for myself much rest."

Throughout chs. 11-12 Mt is engaged in a remarkable presentation of Jesus, remarkable, especially, to readers of Jewish background. Jesus is declared:
   greater than Moses (ch. 5) who wrote the Torah, the Law;
   greater than the Baptist (11:10-11) and Jonah (12:41), both prophets;
   greater than Solomon (12:42), the author of Wisdom literature.

In this clever fashion Mt indicates that Jesus is greater than Torah, Prophets, Wisdom, the divisions of the Hebrew Bible. Jesus stands superior to the whole Old Testament Scripture, just as he is greater, also, than the Jerusalem temple itself (12:7). The work of biblical interpretation and application flowing out of the scholarly school at Jamnia at this time must be judged by the person and the teaching of Jesus, still alive within the Christian community. Yet the element of mystery remains, since the truth of Jesus' being can be accepted only by faith, a faith demonstrated especially by the little ones.

Ch. 12 (very parallel, as we have seen, to Mk 2:23-3:35) keeps giving reactions to Jesus. In special fashion, however, the evangelist's vision focuses in on the Pharisees, a sign, surely, that his Gospel argues especially against this group and the attitude it has taken toward Christians during Mk's own life time. Note:

12:1-8, against Pharisees: feeding the hungry takes precedence over Sabbath Law.

12:9-14, against Pharisees: care for the disabled surpasses Sabbath Law.

12:18-21, Jesus is truly the Servant of Yahweh (Is 42:1-4 which is quoted here is the first Servant Song), but it is the Gentiles to whom he is being preached (v. 18) and who are placing their hope in him (v. 21).

12:22-24, The cure of a man both *blind* and *dumb* leads to *vision* and to a tentative *confession* of Jesus as "Son of David." The Pharisees, however, see in this the action of Beelzebul, prince of demons. This is blasphemy against the Spirit, says 12:31. Just the opposite is true. These miracles are signs that "the kingdom of God has come upon you" (12:28).

12:38-41, Pharisees seek some further sign from Jesus. None will be given except the one supreme sign for Mt's Church, the resurrection.

It is this active resistance to Jesus as Christ that provokes the severe chastisement found in Mt against the Pharisaic party. They are an evil generation (v. 39), less receptive than the pagan Ninivites (v. 41) and a pagan queen (v. 42) for they refuse to accept the new WISDOM that comes from one greater than Solomon (v. 42). Their resistance to the truth opens them to the power of evil (vv. 43-45) while, in their place, rises the true Israel composed of Jesus' family, of those who do the will of his Father who is in heaven (v. 50).

Third Discourse: Kingdom in Mystery, the Parables (ch. 13)

A quick look at our G.P. Index, #90-103, shows us what Mt has done here. Of Mk's three *seed* parables—sower and seed, seed growing secretly, mustard seed—Mt has utilized the first and last, and to them he has added five other parables. These concern the weeds, the leaven, the treasure, the pearl, the net of fish. The leaven is Q material shared almost word for word with Lk (#98), while the other four are M. After the sower and seed story which acts as an introduction, the other six parables fit together as three groups of pairs, each pair with the same general teaching about the kingdom. They thus fall into the following pattern:

(1) Sower and Seed = importance of proper reception of the word of the kingdom (v. 18) and perseverance;

⌐(2) Good Seed & Weeds = mottled character of kingdom which will be purified at the day of judgment;

⌐(3-4) Mustard Seed-Leaven = dynamic force of the kingdom;

∟(5-6) Treasure-Pearl = supreme value of the kingdom;

∟(7) Net of fish = twin to (2).

The discourse is concluded by a reference to the scribe of the kingdom "who brings out of his treasure what is new and what is old" (13:52). This may well be Mt's self-evaluation. He is the kingdom's scribe, a man capable of bringing to the presentation of the good news elements from both the old and the new, from the Jewish past and the Christian present. Reaching back into the Jewish wisdom literature, and with references to Moses, to Jonah, to Solomon and to the temple, he has described Jesus as God's wisdom, as the revelation of God's presence and God's truth among us.

e) BOOK FOUR (13:55-18:35), THE CHURCH

Narrative: (chs. 14-17)

The G.P. Index (#108-136) for this Matthean section demonstrates an almost total dependence on the Markan sequence. Missing here in Mt are only a few bits of Mk: #109, Sending of the Twelve, already used in Mt 9:35; #121, The Blind Man of Bethsaida, which Mt may have indeed wished to omit since Mk intended this story to allude to the disciples' blindness; #130, the Strange Exorcist, which would not fit into Mt's sermon at this point; #132, Concerning Salt, which Mt has already used in 5:13. Notwithstanding this close similarity, Mt has added enough personal touches to the narratives (plus #133-136 in the discourse of ch. 18) to indicate his overall purpose in Book IV. It is at this point in Mt that the Christian community begins to assume its form and structure as Church. The Greek word is *ekklēsia,* which is used in the Greek Old Testament to translate the Hebrew *Qahal,* the assembly of Israel as God's people of both covenant and cult. The following two Old Testament citations speak of God's *Qahal, ekklēsia,* Church, the first in the context of covenant, the second at a moment of cult.

> "And the Lord gave me the two tables of stone written with the finger of God; and on them were all the words which the Lord had spoken with you on the mountain out of the midst of the fire on the day of the *assembly* (ekklēsias)" (Dt 9:10). "Then the king faced about and blessed all Israel while all the *assembly* (ekklēsia) of Israel stood" (1 Kg 8:14).

It is precisely in this section of Mt that the word "Church" is used for the only times in the four Gospels. This word, so frequent in Paul's letters—all of which precede the Gospels in time—is found only in Mt 16:18, but not in the Mk and Lk parallels, and twice more in 18:17. This phenomemon is a strong clue to Mt's intention, to Mt's emphasis at this point.

Also of a certain emphasis and repetition are Mt's presentation of *faith* and of the *loaves.* The element of faith is prominent in 13:58, "And he did not do many works there, because of their unbelief"; in 14:31, "O man of little faith, why did you doubt?"; in 14:33, "And those in the boat worshipped him, saying 'Truly you are the Son of God' "; in 15:28, "O woman, great is your faith! Be it done for you as you desire"; in 15:31, ". . . the crowd wondered, when they saw the dumb speaking, the maimed whole, the lame walking, and the blind seeing; and they glorified the God of Israel"; in 16:16-17, " 'You are the Christ, the Son of the living God.' And Jesus answered him, 'Blessed are you Simon Bar-Jona! For flesh and blood has not revealed this to you, but my Father who is in heaven' "; in 17:20, "Because of your little faith. For truly I say to you, if you have faith as a grain of mustard seed, you will say to this

mountain, 'Move hence to yonder place,' and it will move; and nothing will be impossible to you.''

Together with faith, Mt retains the double story of the multiplication of the loaves
in 14:17ff. and 15:32ff. Lk, as we have seen, drops the second multiplication to save
space. Mt, I suggest, is happy to keep it as he stresses the Church elements most important to him.

Granting the Matthean emphasis on faith and loaves, it is yet another Church
element that Mt seems most intent to build up in this section, namely, Peter. It is
amazing to see how Mt adds to and changes the Markan text to make Peter more
prominent. Some of these changes are small, some are large, all are intentional. The
following stand out:

—in #113, the Walking on the Water, Mt has added vv. 28-31, a passage in which Peter
typifies Christian disciples, both courageous and fearful, and always dependent on the
Lord for salvation;
—in #122, the Confession at Caesarea Philippi, Peter is pronounced rock of the
Church and keeper of the keys of heaven;
—in #124, the Tranfiguration, a tiny change occurs, but it, too, is probably significant.
Where Mk has ''. . . let *us* make three booths,'' Mt's text has Peter saying, ''*I* will make
three booths . . .'';
—in #128, the Temple Tax, we find an M passage (uniquely Matthean) in which Peter
cooperates with Jesus as the disciples of Jesus are declared the free sons of the kingdom;
—finally, in #135, On Reconciliation, Mt assigns to Peter within the sermon proper the
question regarding reconciliation within the Church. This bit of Q material is presented
in the Lukan parallel without any connection to Peter.

What I am suggesting then is that in chs. 14-17 Mt is preparing for his Church
discourse of ch. 18. In this preparation he is strongly controlled by the Markan content
and sequence. Yet he is also creative enough, and free enough, to spotlight three
elements which mean much to his and his community's concept of Church: faith, the
loaves of the Eucharist, the figure of Peter. It may well be that Mt has even divided up
the material so that each main section of these chapters concludes with a Peter incident:
with the Walking on the Water of #113; with Peter's Confession of Faith in #122; and
with the Temple Tax incident of #128.

Fourth Discourse: The Church (ch. 18)

This sermon on the Church may well be the simplest, yet most profound description of Church life ever given. It insists, from beginning to end, on the personal
relationship which Jesus' disciples should have, one with the other. This is a relationship founded on humility, mutual care, concern and correction, unity and forgiveness.
The picture that appears is one of people thoroughly convinced that they are children
of the one Father (''child'' occurs in vv. 2,3,4,5), and brothers and sisters to each other
(''brother'' appears in vv. 15 twice, 21,35).

Mt uses Mk 9:33-37's dispute about greatness (G.P. #129) as the beginning of this sermon: "Who is greatest in the Kingdom of Heaven?" He moves on to #131 regarding temptation, eliminates #130 (partly found in Mt 12:30) and #132 which he has already used, and adds on #133-136. He thereby constructs a series of seven counsels which speak of the relationship which should exist between members of the Church, or—which would make the teaching even stronger—between Church authorities and the other Church members. The relationship, in either case, is based on mutual love and humility. Of this last, the small child is the symbol (18:1-4). Note Mt's second and third uses of "Church" in 18:17 and a final mention of Peter in 18:21. This presents a series of seven "Church counsels":

1) counsel to childlike humility (vv. 1-4);
2) counsel to special care of the weak (v. 5);
3) counsel against scandal: scandal of the weak, in the world, of self (6-9);
4) counsel to apostolic spirit concerning the lost sheep (10-14);
5) counsel to fraternal correction (15-18);
6) counsel to common prayer and unity (19-20), concluding with "there am I in the midst of them," reminding us of Emmanuel, God with us, with whom the Gospel began;
7) counsel to complete, unfailing forgiveness, contrasted perhaps against the attitude of Lamech in Gn 4:23-24. This forgiveness is illustrated by the uniquely Matthean parable of the unjust steward who failed to forgive his brother from his heart (21-35). The topic is initiated by Peter (note difference in Lk 17:3-4 in G.P. #134) who, himself, denied Jesus three times.

f) BOOK FIVE (chs. 19-25), THE END

Narrative, plus the Seven Woes (chs. 19-23)

Our G.P. Index shows us that these five chapters of Mt are almost identical to the corresponding material in Mk, chs. 10-12. Mt has used all the Markan account (except #212, the widow's mite story, which perhaps for Mt does not seem to fit the somber mood of these chapters) and has added a number of incidents which he considers appropriate: the parables of the laborers in the vineyard (G.P. #190: cf. Is 5:1-7), of the two sons (#203) and of the marriage feast (#205), plus the lament over Jerusalem (#211). All will prepare for the grim discourse of chs. 24-25 and for the passion story which will follow. A number of common points of interest in chs. 19-23 tie the whole into a loose unity. These points are:

1) steps along the journey. 19:1 notes the beginning of Jesus' journey from Galilee to Jerusalem. He leaves Galilee for the district of Judea beyond the Jordan, i.e., to the east of the Jordan river. In 20:17 "Jesus was going up to Jerusalem." In 20:29 Mt states that it was "as they went out of Jericho" that the two blind men were cured. In 21:1 "they drew near to Jerusalem" and in 21:10 "he entered Jerusalem." This is one of the features of these chapters, *Jesus' sacrificial pilgrimage to Jerusalem*. We have already seen it as Mk's "Way to the Cross" theme. It will be even more pronounced in Lk.

2) the strong note of crisis that pervades this material as Jesus goes up to his death. Reference is made to this death (20:18-19; 21:38-39, 46), as well as to the end of individual's lives (19:16-17, 21, 23-25, 28-29; 20:8, 21; 22:13, 30-32), to the punishment of Jesus' murderers (21:41-44), to the ruin of Jerusalem and the temple (22:7; 23:38).

3) the controversies of Jesus in Jerusalem. According to the Synoptic arrangement this is the first time that Jesus visits the Holy City during his ministry. (Knowledge of previous visits, however, may be insinuated in 23:37.) The antagonism he arouses there, which is spread out in more leisurely fashion in John's Gospel with its many visits to Jerusalem (cf. Jn 2:13; 5:1; 7:10; 10:22) must be compressed in the Synoptics into this one section. We find these chapters, consequently, overflowing with *controversy* stories which serve to prepare the reader for a hatred against Jesus bitter enough to put him to death. There is a long list of these encounters.

19:3-9	with Pharisees	on divorce
21:12-16	with priests and scribes	regarding the temple cleansing and the children crying "Hosanna"
21:23-27	with priests, elders and Pharisees (v. 45)	regarding Jesus' authority
21:28-32	with priests, elders and Pharisees	concerning the two sons
21:33-46	with priests, elders and Pharisees	on the murder of the vineyard owner's son
22:1-10	with priests, elders and Pharisees	regarding the marriage feast
22:15-22	with the Pharisees	concerning taxes to Caesar
22:23-33	with the Sadducees	on resurrection
22:35-40	with the Pharisees	regarding the great commandment
22:41-46	with the Pharisees	on the sonship of the Christ
23:1-36	which give the "Seven Woes"	against the scribes and Pharisees.

4) a reversal of God's election. A number of passages indicate the opening of the kingdom to unexpected guests, a turning-upside-down of the expected outline of God's plan of salvation. Thus:

19:30—"But many that are first will be last, and the last first."

20:14, 16—"Take what belongs to you and go; I choose to give to this last as I give to you . . . So the last will be first, and the first last."

21:31—"Truly I say to you, the tax collectors and the harlots go into the kingdom of God before you."

21:41, 43—"He will put those wretches to a miserable death, and let out the vineyard to other tenants who will give him the fruits in their season . . . . Therefore I tell you, the kingdom of God will be taken away from you and given to a nation producing the fruits of it."

22:8-9—"The wedding is ready, but those invited were not worthy. Go therefore to the thoroughfares, and invite to the marriage feast as many as you find.''

5) a proclamation of Jesus as both Son of David, the Jewish Messiah (20:30-31; 21:9, 15; 22:42), and as Lord (22:43-45).

6) the all-importance of love. Important as the Law is to Jewish Mt it is superceded by love. Mt's most impressive statement of this still awaits the reader (25:31-46) but he has now presented this doctrine in various parts of his Gospel. Confer 5:43-48, a vigorous statement of love, even for enemies; 19:19 where Mt adds to Mk's text (G.P. #189) ''You shall love your neighbor as yourself''; 22:38-40 where Mt notes, in contrast to Mk (G.P. #208) that the second commandment, love of neighbor, *is like love of God* and that on these two commandments of love depend the whole law and the prophets.

Perhaps I should say something at this point about ch. 23 which has long caused difficulty to those interested in an exact division of Mt's Gospel. Is it the beginning of the final discourse which, consequently, would include chs. 23-25? Is it independent of the final discourse, and to be attached to chs. 19-22? Is it another discourse, thus upsetting our proposed Christian Torah—the five books—exposition of Mt? My own opinion is that it is not a separated sermon, running the total up to six, mainly because the sermons in Mt are teaching directed to the disciples and the crowds interested in Jesus. Ch. 23 is quite different. It is—almost in its entirety—a series of condemnations directed against the scribes and Pharisees, independent therefore from the ''sermon pattern'' of Mt and to be attached to chs. 19-22 as preparatory to the final sermon of chs. 24-25. In this sense it is a continuation of the controversies between Jesus and the Jerusalem authorities so prevalent in this preparatory section.

Fifth Discourse: The Ends (chs. 24-25)

These are two heavy chapters, filled with concern for the future and held together linguistically by the repetition of such key words as ''those days'' (24:15-31), ''day'' and ''hour'' (24:32-51), and ''watch'' (25:1-13). The atmosphere is fraught with tension and expectation. We must judge that times are difficult for Mt's community. Suffering has fallen upon the group, some have fallen away, others have betrayed the Church, love in many has grown cold (24:9-12). Added to these personal difficulties are world-shaking events—the sacrilege standing in the holy place (a reference to Dn 9:37; 11:31; 12:11 which the Gospel believes fulfilled when the banners of the Roman legionnaires were brought into the temple precincts and the emperors were worshipped there), wars, and rumors of wars.

The context out of which Mt is writing seems clear enough. What is difficult to grasp clearly is precisely what Mt is describing in each section of these two chapters. You will notice that in 24:3 (G.P. #213) he has changed the question posed to Jesus by the disciples in Mark. Where Mk's question (Mk 13:4) can be limited to the destruction of the temple (as it definitely is in the Lukan parallel of 21:7) Mt has expanded the question to include three not necessarily identical events. In Mt's phrasing—with my clarifications in parentheses—the disciples ask: ''Tell us, when will this be (the destruction of the temple), and what will be the sign of your coming (Jesus' parousia, his second coming) and of the close of the age (the end of the world)?'' Mt has thus created a tri-pronged question.

It appears that he has also attempted a tri-pronged answer. Verses 4-14 seem to speak of the end of the world, to take place only after the gospel of the kingdom has been preached to all nations (v. 14). Verses 15-22 center on the temple abomination and destruction, an event which presumably has already taken place as Mt writes this Gospel. And verses 23-31 speak of the coming of the Son of Man. Yet Mt does not distinguish these three events neatly as becomes evident in verses 32ff. where all three seem to be lumped together. Historically we know that Jerusalem, and its temple, and that peculiar structuring of the Jewish world that depended on city, temple, priesthood, and sacrifices were destroyed in the year 70 A.D. by the Roman invaders. Historically we know that this material, unreconstituted, good-evil world of ours still exists. Theologically we Christians believe that Jesus has come again in one sense—in his resurrected life, in his Spirit, in his Church and his saving sacraments—and that, in another sense, he is still awaited. This knowledge of ours gives us a distinct advantage over Mt himself. Views into the eschatological future are always dim.

Notwithstanding this necessary limitation, Mt has left us some precious material in this sermon. It has given us seven parables of warning, a caution to live life a bit on the edge of our seats, since we never really know when the world, or at least our individual personal world, will reach its end. These parables derive from a mixture of Mk, Q and M, from all the sources out of which Mt has created his Gospel. Thus:

24:32-33 (Mk)	—Fig Tree;
24:37-41 (Q)	—Days of Noah;
24:42-44 (Q)	—Householder and Thief;
24:45-51 (Q)	—Faithful and Wise Servant;
25:1-13 (M)	—Ten Maidens;
25:14-30 (Q)	—Servants with Talents;
25:31-46 (M)	—Final Judgment.

Mt, as was noted previously, has already insisted on the primacy of the love commandment in 5:43-48; 19:19; 22:38-40. It is at this present point in his Gospel, however, in the grim warning concerning the end of Jerusalem, the coming of Jesus, and the end of the world that happily enough the Gospel's teaching on love reaches its peak. The sole criterion for judgment in 25:31-46 is LOVE. (This is a striking and unexpected parallel to the teaching in John's Gospel that love does away with judgment.) As the judgment is a judgment for all (v. 32's ''all the nations'') so, too, the criterion is universal. As God is Father of all, so are we all brothers and sisters to the Father's ''beloved son'' (3:17; 17:5). Whatever we do or do not do to Jesus' brothers and sisters, we do or deny to him.

''When Jesus had finished *all these sayings*'' (26:1) is, this time, Mt's ending to the whole of Jesus' public teaching, the conclusion to the five books of Christian Torah, the inspiration of what Mt terms so frequently the ''Kingdom of heaven.''

g) SOLEMN CONCLUSION: (chs. 26-28): PASSION, DEATH, RESURREC-
TION, COMMISSION

A quick look at our G.P. Index reveals that Mt and Mk have identical sequences
through incidents #231-251 (twenty-two passages) except for Mt's unique reference to
the death of Judas in #243. And often enough they have the same wording. Yet even
here there are Matthean touches which differentiate this evangelist from Mk.

Mt has special references to Caiphas at 26:3 and 26:57.

He also builds up with interesting details and Old Testament references the story
of Judas. In 26:15 Judas is paid thirty pieces of silver, a first reference to the passage in
Zech 11:12 where thirty silver shekels are cast into the treasury in the house of the Lord.
In 26:25 Judas asks Jesus, "Is it I, Lord?" and receives an affirmative answer. In 26:50
Jesus responds to Judas' kiss in Gethsemane with "Friend, why are you here?" And in
27:3-10 we are given a description of Judas' tragic end, painted in colors derived from
Old Testament passages. This paragraph must be read against Zech 11:12 which refers
to the thirty pieces of silver, and against Jer 19 with its references to the potter's flask,
the potsherd gate, the valley of slaughter and the impending doom awaiting the city of
Jerusalem. It must also be read against 2 Sam 17:24 where Ahithophel, traitor to
David, went off to his home "and hanged himself." Judas, traitor to the new David,
says Mt, dies a traitor's death.

He also provides special material on Pilate and his family. Pilate's wife appears in
27:19, and his symbolic, but ineffectual, hand washing is described in 27:24-25.

There is also a special insistence in Mt on Jesus as Son of God. This appears in
27:40, 43.

The story of the guards at the tomb is a special contribution by Mt in 27:62-66.
This will combine with 28:11-15, the bribing of the soldiers, to answer what must have
been a common anti-Christian explanation of the empty tomb (theft by Christians)
which was used against the Church of Mt's own time.

It is interesting to note what little pieces of Mk that Mt has omitted. The account
of the lad who lost his shirt in the garden (G.P. #240: Mk 14:51-52) shows up missing in
Mt. Clearly this detail must have been of interest to Mk (an autobiographical detail,
perhaps?), but not to Mt. And the mention of "the father of Alexander and Rufus"
(G.P. #248: Mk 15:21) in connection with Simon of Cyrene, also disappears in Mt, *If*
this Rufus is the same as that mentioned in Rom 16:13, and *if* that chapter 16 was
actually destined for Rome, and *if* Mk was written in Rome, then it is apparent why Mk
had a special interest in Rufus and his brother. But there are a lot of *ifs* here!

Of special interest is the Matthean addition in 27:51b-53. Into the description of
Jesus' death come an earthquake, the opening of tombs, and the resurrection of the
saints. This certainly seems to be a statement of an eschatological irruption of the
divinity into the world, and a strong hint, to say the least, that Mt views Jesus'
death—as he will the resurrection—as the beginning of a new age, a new world.

The final chapter of Mt is very different from that of Mk. The story of the empty
tomb is similar enough in both, though Mt lacks the anointing motif found in Mk, and
has inserted an eschatological description of an earthquake and an angel of flashing
appearance. But the big difference is between the conclusion in Mk 16:8 (what follows
in Mk 16:9-20 is a later addition) and that of Mt 28:8-20. Mt combines the Markan note

of fear with joy, and then follows with a brief appearance of the risen Lord in Jerusalem.

Completely unique to Mt, and basic to the theology of his entire Gospel, is the Great Commission of 28:16-20. Dn 7:14 had spoken of a Son of Man to whom "was given dominion and glory and kingdom, that all peoples, nations, and languages should serve him; his dominion is an everlasting dominion, which shall not pass away, and his kingdom one that shall not be destroyed." Mt's Commission identifies this Son of Man as Jesus, Son of David, Lord, Son of God, the new Moses, the new Israel. To him has been given all authority on heaven and earth. And to his disciples does he now transfer it, commissioning them to evangelize all nations, baptizing them in the name of the Trinity, and teaching with the very authority which he has received from the Father. The new Israel, says Mt, is now the Christian Church. And Jesus is its Emmanuel—God with us—always, to the close of the age. Mt binds his Gospel within covers bearing the title *Emmanuel* (1:23; 28:20) and, with the same motion, moves the Church off to its mission to all nations. The pagan Magi came to Emmanuel; Emmanuel, through the Church, now goes out to the Magi. And this—for all Christians—is, indeed, the good news of the Lord.

3. Author

The Gospel itself does not identify its author. Its attribution to Matthew is an ancient tradition which can be traced back to both Papias, in the first half of the second century, and to Irenaeus some 50 years later.

Modern scholarship has studied the interests and writing patterns of the author and agrees (with some rare exceptions) that he was a Jewish Christian, strongly in favor of the mission to the Gentiles with which the book both begins (Magi of ch. 2) and ends (Great Commission of 28:18-20). His interest in his Jewish roots is evident in his genealogy with its emphasis on Abraham and David, in his affirmation of the Law and Prophets in 5:17-19 (uniquely Matthean), and in his willingness in 10:5-6 to record Jesus' own preaching pattern, a mission to "the lost sheep of the house of Israel." This Jewish emphasis is deliberately balanced by his recounting of the amazing praise given to the Gentile centurion in 8:10-12, of the warning to the Jerusalem authorities in 21:43, and of the solemn commission to enroll all nations with a ceremonial initiation different from circumcision (28:18-20). If 13:52 is not Mt's conscious self-description, it certainly appears to fit him perfectly: "Therefore every scribe who has been trained for the kingdom of heaven is like a householder who brings out of his treasure what is new and what is old."

This author can hardly be Matthew, the apostle, an eyewitness to Jesus' public life. He is far too dependent on Mk for that. Yet Matthew the apostle may have been an important source for this writing. Two pieces of information point in this direction. Papias spoke of Mt as having written in Hebrew—better, Aramaic—the *logia,* the *sayings* of Jesus. This may indicate that the apostle stands behind the Q source, and that Mt was so named because it represented a combining of Mk and Mt's Q. A second oddity that ties the Gospel of Mt to the apostle is its striking change of Mk in G.P. #53. Where Mk 2:14, followed by Lk 5:27, speaks of Levi the tax collector, this same individual is called Matthew in Mt's Gospel, some indication, certainly, that the author had a special interest in Mt, the apostle. The conclusion to all of this, finally, is that the author is unknown, but that he was a Jewish-Christian dependent on both Mk and Q, which latter *may* have stemmed from the apostle Matthew.

4. *Place and Time*

Here, too, we end up with uncertainties. A sufficient period of time must have elapsed between Mk and Mt to allow for a copy of Mk to have reached the author of Mt. A similar period of time is required for the center at Jamnia to have developed into an authoritative group whose decisions and interpretations could have been at odds with the beliefs of Jewish Christians. The controversies against the Pharisees in Mt are so animated (cf. ch. 23) that they must echo a Matthean Church engaged in passionate conflict with Pharisaic Judaism. We can guess at a date close to 85 A.D.

And place? The Gospel itself witnesses to a community which still prizes its Jewish roots and yet is wide open with enthusiasm to the Gentiles. It also witnesses to an interest in cities, utilizing the word some twenty-seven times in its text. Scholars lean to a territory where a mixed Jewish-Gentile Church was possible, and where such a community would have been in contact with the Jewish synagogues. Syria is a distinct possibility, and, if a city must be chosen, Antioch is a likely choice. It housed a heavy Jewish population and had been a thriving Jewish-Gentile Christian center from the earliest days of the Church, the inspiration and springboard for the missionary endeavors of Paul and Barnabas. Some reinforcement for this choice comes from the reference to Syria in Mt 4:24, a reference which is unique to Mt: "So his fame spread throughout all Syria . . ." Another support comes from the fact that Ignatius of *Antioch* (at the end of the first century) gives what appear to be the earliest quotes from Mt. Mt 3:15 appears in Ignatius' Letter to the Smyrneans I, 1 and Mt 10:16 is found in his Letter to Polycarp, II, 2.

5. *Intended Audience: Some Theological Contributions*

Mt's openness to the Gentile mission, with baptism replacing circumcision (28:18-20), means that he must also have visualized Gentile readers of his Gospel text. Yet it also seems probable that he intended his writing mainly for Jewish Christians and other interested Jews. The problem which keeps surfacing is the relationship of Law, Mosaic Law, to Christian living. This is obviously a *Jewish*-Christian problem. In this we are reminded of Mt's predecessor, the Jewish Paul of Tarsus, two of whose letters, Galatians and Romans, are given over to the same problem. How does the Law affect Jewish Christians, and what authority does the Jewish center at Jamnia have on Mt and his Jewish companions? To say that Mt's answer is perfectly clear and perfectly balanced would be as incorrect as to assert the same for Paul. Both men struggled with the problem which was for them as vital as life itself, for it was indeed their lives which were intimately involved. Both left some strings untied, some dangling ends. And both, in their struggles for solutions, made enormous contributions to Christian theology.

I'd like to conclude this treatment by stressing a few of Matthew's theological assertions.

a) Law

Mt, a Jewish Christian, cannot simply dismiss Mosaic Law since it was God's will, God's word. YET

(i) something new has happened. The "until all is accomplished" of Mt 5:18—"... till heaven and earth pass away, not an iota, not a dot, will pass from the law *until all is accomplished*"—has taken place, witnessed to by the eschatological signs of Jesus' death and resurrection. Note Mt's special insistence: "And behold, the curtain of the temple was torn in two, from top to bottom; and the earth shook, and the rocks were split; the tombs also were opened, and many bodies of the saints who had fallen asleep were raised, and coming out of the tombs after his resurrection they went into the holy city and appeared to many" (27:51-53). "And behold, there was a great earthquake; for an angel of the Lord descended from heaven and came and rolled back the stone, and sat upon it. His appearance was like lightning, and his rainment white as snow. And for fear of him the guards trembled and became like dead men" (28:2-4).

This eschatological newness weakens the overwhelming authority of the Law as absolute rule of life, and can even dispense with so essential an element of the Mosaic Law as circumcision. Baptism—equally available to both sexes—takes its place in Mt 28:19.

(ii) All law has a new principle of interpretation, and that is love. Law is to be interpreted by love. If Mt still insists on the necessity of law, he does so in a new climate of openness to Gentiles, and with a new rule of interpretation.

(iii) One might even say that with Jesus' death and resurrection the eschaton, the final period, has arrived for Mt, dissolving the during-Christ's-lifetime limitations of territory and people and Mosaic Law. This Christian freedom is represented in Mt 28:18-20. It is in Jesus that his disciples will find God's presence and teaching and authority. And he transmits all this to them, sending them out to all lands and to all peoples to enlist all nations in his Father's kingdom through baptism. And this till the very end of the end.

(iv) Even with regard to particular positive laws God, rather than being demanding, is loving and gracious and merciful. Mt 9:13 and 12:7 apply to the practical problems of eating with tax collectors, and of both feeding and curing on the Sabbath the gentle quote from Hosea: "I desire mercy and not sacrifice" (Hos 6:6).

b) Love

The constant emphasis which Mt—the superior organizer, Churchman, conservative—gives to the necessity of love is amazing and inspiring.

(i) 5:43-48 is derived from Q and insists on love for enemies and prayers for persecutors. This is what Christian perfection is because this is what God is, God our Father who "makes his sun rise on the evil and on the good, and sends rain on the just and on the unjust."

(ii) 19:19 contains a Matthean addition not found in the parallels of Mk and Lk. To the negative commandments Mt adds one positive statement that includes them all: "You shall love your neighbor as yourself."

(iii) 22:36-40 has two Matthean peculiarities missing in the parallels. The first is v.

39: *"And a second is like it,* you shall love your neighbor as yourself," thus bringing love of God and love of neighbor into a rough balance. And in v. 40, Mt notes that "all the law and the prophets" depend on these two commandments of love.

(iv) 25:31-46, the last judgment scene, is Mt's glorious conclusion to the whole of Jesus' teaching. Entrance into the kingdom depends on what we have done or not done for the indigent, the least of Jesus' brethren.

c) Eschatology

The subject of Mt's eschatology is complex, perhaps because Mt himself did not see it all that clearly. The text of 5:18-19, "For truly I say to you, till heaven and earth pass away, not an iota, not a dot, will pass from the law until all is accomplished. Whoever then relaxes one of the least of these commandments and teaches men so, shall be called least in the kingdom of heaven . . ." appears to envision a continuation of law until heaven and earth pass away in a final apocalyptic blast. Yet "until all is accomplished" may well refer to Jesus' death and resurrection, and "the least of these commandments" are those of the *kingdom of heaven.* Again in Mt 24:3 Jesus is asked: "When will this be (destruction of Jerusalem) and what will be the sign of your coming and of the close of the age?" The answer is given in dependence on Mk, and is ambiguous. The Gospel must first be preached throughout the whole world (24:14). The desolating sacrilege must first be seen standing in the holy place (24:15). False Christs and false prophets must first arise (24:24). No one except the Father knows either the day or the hour (24:36). And yet "he is near, at the very gates" (24:33) and "this generation will not pass away till all these things take place" (24:34).

Mt certainly believes in a futuristic eschatology. But does he also believe that in some way the kingdom has already arrived in Christ, that the last days have already arrived? The answer appears to be Yes. In both 27:51-53 and 28:2-3 Mt adds to Mk eschatological indications, epiphany language, i.e., language type-cast for the irruption of God into the world. Earth shakes, rocks split, tombs open, saints arise, an angel of the Lord descends, guards tremble and freeze in fear. The new aeon has arrived. And so Mt's final words emphasize, not the future coming of the Son of Man, but the abiding presence of Emmanuel, God with us, through whom and in whom the entrance into the kingdom is open to all the nations.

Chapter Seven

The Good News According to Luke

1. Introduction: Lk's Gospel and his Acts of the Apostles

a) Although our concentration here will be on Lk's Gospel, we must deal initially with the fact that Lk has given us a two-volume work, the Gospel and the Acts of the Apostles, both intimately related the one to the other. This intended relationship becomes obvious when we note (1) the over-all parallel structure in both, (2) the manner in which Lk has tied together the ending of the Gospel with the beginning of Acts, and (3) the specific and striking parallels in detail which can be found in the two books. Lk intends that these two volumes be read, prayed, and studied together.

(1) The Over-All Parallel Structures. Hopefully the following brief outline will make this general structure obvious.

Good News of Jesus = GOSPEL	*Good News of Church = ACTS*
(Movement of Spirit-led Jesus)	(Movement of Spirit-led Church)
(from Galilee to Jerusalem)	(from Jerusalem to Rome)
—Prologue to Theophilus (1:1-4)	—Prologue to Theophilus (1:1)
1. The Spirit comes (1:5-2:52)	1. The Spirit comes (1:2-2:47)
2. Baptism, temptation, *Galilee* (3:1-9:50)	2. Baptism (2:38), *Jerusalem* (3:1-7:60)
3. *Galilee to Jerusalem* (9:51-19:44)	3. *Jerusalem to Rome* (8:1-28:16)
4. *Jerusalem* (19:45-24:53)	4. *Rome* (28:17-31)

The Gospel moves the story of Jesus from Galilee to Jerusalem. Marching in step, Acts moves the story of the Church from Jerusalem to Rome.

(2) Gospel-Ending = Beginning of Acts

Lk has also tied together, and with skill, the end of the Gospel and the start of Acts. Note the following parallels:

Luke 24	*Acts 1*
24:33-34, 36 The risen Christ appears to Simon and to the eleven apostles.	1:3 The risen Christ appears to the apostles whom he has chosen.
24:36-43 Jesus proves that it is he by offering to be touched and by eating before them.	1:3 "To them he presented himself alive after his passion by many proofs . . . ."
24:49 "And behold, I send the promise of my Father upon you; but stay in the city until you are clothed with power from on high."	1:4 "And while staying with them he charged them not to depart from Jerusalem but to wait for the promise of the Father . . ."
24:47-48 ". . . and that repentance and forgiveness of sins would be preached in his name to all nations, beginning from Jerusalem. You are witnesses of these things."	1:8b ". . . and you shall be my witnesses in Jerusalem and in all Judea and Samaria and to the end of the earth."
24:51-52 ". . . and he parted from them. And they returned to Jerusalem."	1:9, 12 ". . . as they were looking on, he was lifted up, and a cloud took him out of their sight . . . . Then they returned to Jerusalem."

(3) Detailed Parallels Found in Lk's Gospel and Acts

Here I would like to limit myself to those parallels which seem most striking, but advising the reader that many others could be offered. Some are so remarkable that it is impossible to believe that they are not intentional.

Gospel	*Acts*
1:1-4 Preface to Theophilus	1:1-5 Preface to Theophilus
3:22 Spirit descends in physical form	2:1-13 Spirit descends in physical form
4:16-30 Inaugural sermon which previews the whole of Jesus' ministry	2:14-40 Inaugural sermon which previews the whole story of Acts
5:17-26 Lame man healed by Jesus	3:1-10 Lame man healed by Jesus' name
7:1-10 A centurion sends men to Jesus asking that he come to his home	10:1-23 A centurion sends men to Peter asking that he come to his home
7:11-17 Widow of Nain and resurrection: Jesus says "Arise" and the dead son "sat up."	9:36-43 Widows and resurrection of Tabitha: Peter says "Rise" and the woman "sat up."
9:51-19:28 Jesus makes passion journey to Jerusalem	19:21-21:17 Paul makes passion journey to Jerusalem
22:54 A mob seizes Jesus	21:30 A mob seizes Paul

22:63f. Jesus slapped	23:2 Paul slapped
22:66; 23:1, 8, 13 Four trials of Jesus before Sanhedrin, Pilate, Herod, Pilate	Chs. 23, 24, 25, 26 Four trials of Paul before Sanhedrin, Felix, Festus, Herod Agrippa II
23:4, 14, 22 Pilate declares Jesus innocent three times	23:29; 25:55; 26:31 Paul declared innocent three times
23:18 "Away with this man!"	21:36 "Away with him!"

Luke has surely marched both of his books to the same drummer. One scholarly opinion is that both were outlined first, with details fitted in afterwards. Something like this must be postulated to explain the precisioned parallelism which Lk has created. One result of this intimate tying together of the two works is that Lk's Gospel must be studied in itself to identify his overall composition, must also be studied in relation to Mk and Mt to learn from the differences, and must finally be studied with an eye on Acts since Lk's two volumes help to mutually clarify each other.

Take, for example, the story of the centurion in Lk 7:1-10. In comparison with Mt 8:5-13 it has been noted for centuries that whereas in Mt the centurion himself goes to Jesus with his request for help, in Lk the centurion *sends elders to Jesus.* In the days when it was considered necessary to harmonize all differences in the Gospels this provoked a problem. Did the centurion go personally to Jesus, or did he send a delegation? But, perhaps, the real explanation of the difference comes from Lk's attention to the parallel story in Acts 10 where another centurion, Cornelius, *sends men to Peter.* The Gospel story may have been rearranged to form a perfect parallel to its twin in Acts. This would also mean that the Acts' story would have been present to Lk, maybe even in writing, as Lk composed the corresponding part of the Gospel.

b) GEOGRAPHY = THEOLOGY IN LK-ACTS

Lk's geography moves the good news of and about Jesus *to Jerusalem, center of the Jewish world,* and subsequently *to Rome, center of the Gentile world.* But more than geography is involved here. During Lk's life-time the good news has, in fact, passed from the Jewish world (symbolized by Jerusalem) to the Gentile world (symbolized by Rome), for the Church has become predominantly non-Jewish. Lk's is a tale of two cities, with symbolic overtones. An important part of Lk's task is to certify that this transition has been legitimate, according to God's will. He does this (1) by insisting on the continuous presence and guidance of the Spirit, and (2) by reference to scriptural passages which speak of God's future gift of his saving light to the Gentiles. (Cf. Is 2:1-3; 42:6; 49:6, noting the intimate connection of Is 49:6 to Acts 1:8 and 13:47.) Lk stresses this move to the Gentile world:

—at the beginning of Jesus' ministry (3:6, ". . . *all flesh* shall see the salvation of God"; 4:25-27, the prophets bring salvation to a pagan man and woman);
—at its ending (24:47, ". . . repentance and forgiveness of sins should be preached in his name to all nations . . .");
—at the beginning of Acts (1:8, "You shall be my witnesses in Jerusalem and in all Judea and Samaria and to the end of the earth.");
—at the middle of Acts (13:47, "I have set you to be a light for the Gentiles, that you

may bring salvation to the uttermost parts of the earth.'');
—at its ending (28:28, ''Let it be known to you then that this salvation of God has been sent to the Gentiles.'').

Looked at individually, both books begin and end with the same theme. Considered as a unit, as one two-volume work, the beginning and ending are the same, with an enormous emphasis in the middle where the two parts tie together. It is hard to doubt that Lk's central theme, therefore, is *Light to the Gentiles.*

Lk's geographical movement, Jerusalem to Rome, is the external pattern of Lk's theological thought. The word of God has gone out to all the world and, in the process, guided by the Spirit and foreshadowed in the Old Testament scriptures, has passed from Jerusalem to Rome, from the Jewish world to the Gentile. In this tale of two cities, the movement is the message.

c) Together these two volumes constitute about twenty-seven percent of the whole New Testament and form its largest single coherent block, quantitatively larger than the total of Paul's letters. Often considered the most beautiful book in the world, Lk's version of the good news is particularly rich in theological themes. It is a Gospel of:

(i) gentleness, mercy and mildness (6:36; 7:13; 23:24; 23:43);
(ii) joy (1:14, 28, 44, 47, 58; 2:10, 13-14; 10:17; 13:17; 19:6; 15:1-32; 28:52);
(iii) great pardons (7:36-50; 15:11-32; 19:1-10; 23:34; 23:43);
(iv) infinite mercy to
    sinners (7:36-50; 15:3-7, 8-10, 11-32; 18:10-14; 19:10),
    tax-collectors (3:12; 15:27-30; 7:29, 34; 15:1; 18:10-13; 19:1-10),
    Samaritans (10:29-37; 17:16),
    Gentiles (2:32; 3:6, 38; 4:25-27; 7:9; 13:29; 24:47);
(v) women (1:35, 41; 7:11-17, 36-50; 8:1-3; 10:38-42; 21:1-4; 23:27; 23:55-56; 24:1-11);
(vi) prayer (3:21-23; 6:12-13; 9:18-20, 28-31; 22:41-43; 23:46);
(vii) the Spirit (1:15, 35, 41, 67, 80; 2:25-27; 3:16, 22; 4:1, 11, 18; 10:21; 11:13; 12:10, 12).

2. *Process of Lk's Gospel*

a) INFANCY NARRATIVE (1:1-2:52)

Lk's two infancy chapters are to a great extent his own production and form an extremely artistic presentation divided into seven scenes. Each scene centers on one incident, is terminated by the departure of some or all of the principal characters from the stage, and frequently includes a song, a canticle or hymn of varying length. One gets the feeling that one is reading the script for a sacred stage play, rich in theological content. Thus:

Incident	Departure	Song
1) Zechariah-Elizabeth (1:5-25)	''and he went to his home'' (1:23) and ''she hid herself'' (1:24)	None

2) Annunciation to Mary (1:26-38)	"angel departed" (1:38)	None
3) Visitation (1:39-56)	"Mary . . . returned . . . home" (1:56)	Mary's Magnificat
4) Birth of Baptist (1:57-80)	"he was in wilderness" (1:80)	Zechariah's Benedictus
5) Birth of Jesus (2:1-20)	"shepherds returned" (2:20)	Angels' song
6) Circumcision-presentation (2:21-40)	"they returned into Galilee" (2:39)	Simeon's song
7) Loss-finding in temple (2:41-52)	"And he went down with them" (2:51)	None

These seven scenes, moreover, are laid out in two pair of stories, that of *the annunciations* (to Zechariah and Mary) and that of *the births* (of the Baptist and Jesus). In this fashion Lk constructs a parallel between the Baptist and Jesus, but both the quality and the quantity of content emphasize the superiority of Mary's son.

Twin ANNUNCIATION Stories

Scene 1. Zechariah (1:5-56)		Scene 2. Mary
1:5-10	Details about parents of the child	1:26-27
1:11	Angel (Gabriel) appears to parent	1:28
1:12	Parent is frightened by the visit	1:29
1:13a	Angel reassures the parent	1:30a
1:13b-17	Annunciation to the parent	1:30b-33
1:18	Question asked by the parent	1:34
1:19	Response of the angel	1:35
1:20	Sign given by angel to the parent	1:36-37
1:21-25	Reaction of parent(s) and departure	1:38

Scene 3. Sequel: the Visitation (1:39-56). Persons, dialogue, canticle, exit.

Twin BIRTH Stories

Scene 4. Birth of John (1:57-80) Scene 5. Birth of Jesus (2:1-20)
Scene 6. Circumcision-presentation (2:21-40)

1:57	Birth of the child	2:1-7
1:58	Joy at news of the birth	2:8-20
1:59a	Circumcision of the child	2:21
1:59b-66	Manifestation of the child	2:22-38
1:67-79	Canticle of thanksgiving	2:29-32
1:80	Growth of the child, expressed in identical words: "And the child grew and became strong. . . ."	2:40

Scene 7. Sequel: Jesus in Temple (2:41-52). Persons, dialogue, exit, contemplation, growth.

One thing that strikes the eye and consciousness here is an almost total difference from Mt's infancy narrative. Lk presents the story with Mary—rather than Joseph as in Mt—as the main character. He lacks any reference to the Magi, to Herod's slaughter of the children, to a flight into Egypt. He has his own unique apparition to the shepherds. It is hard to imagine that either Mt or Lk has a copy of the other's Gospel.

These two initial chapters of Lk are amazingly rich in verbal echoes of Old Testament psalmic poetry. To verify this, simply look at the footnote references at the bottom of G.P., p. 5. This is especially true of the numerous songs—of Mary, of Zechariah, of the angels, of Simeon. That of Simeon (2:29-32) is of special interest after our contact with the Suffering Servant theme so important for Mark. In Simeon's song is clearly discerned the servant theology in poetic form: the servant bringing salvation, "a light for revelation to the Gentiles, and for glory to thy people Israel," followed by division and contradiction and concluding, surprisingly enough, not with the passion of Jesus but with the compassion of his mother.

The narrative mvoes Jesus twice to the city of Jerusalem and its temple (presentation, and the finding in the temple), a foreshadowing of the basic movement of the Gospel which places such unique stress (chs. 9-19) on Jesus' final journey to the Holy City. Lk seems especially sensitive to Mal 3:1, "Behold I send my messenger to prepare the way before me, and *the Lord whom you seek will suddenly come to his temple* . . ." We can note, too, the similar movement in Lk's temptation story (4:1-13 = G.P. #8) which has the Matthean sequence of second and third temptations in reverse order. In Lk the temptation narrative, like the Gospel itself, concludes in Jerusalem.

(b) TEMPTATION AND GALILEAN MINISTRY (3:1-9:50 = G.P. #1-130)

(i) 3:1-6:19. What is obvious here from the G.P. Index is Lk's willingness to follow almost exactly Mk's sequence and in the sequence to accept almost entirely the Markan incidents. Where Mt moves away from Mk to organize his sermons in chs. 5-7 and 10 and to bolster his narrative in ch. 11, Lk stays right with Mk. When he finally moves from Mk he will do so in extreme fashion, but throughout 3:1-6:19 he and Mk proceed hand in hand. Lk has incorporated almost two-thirds of Mk's text into his own Gospel.

But Lk also shows some flashes of independence, even here. For one thing, he dates the beginning of his good news to the fifteenth year of Tiberius Caesar, who reigned from 14-37 A.D. This would place the beginning of the ministry about 28 A.D. Jesus, born before Herod's death in 4 B.C., would have been about thirty-three years old. Lk 3:23 puts it in rough figures, "about thirty years of age."

Lk bunches half of his material on John the Baptist into 3:2-20 (the other half will be found in 7:18-35, with an added note on John's death in 9:7-9), adds #2 (fine example of Q, including an allusion to universal salvation), #3 and, surprisingly, #5, John's imprisonment (at Machaerus, a fortress in the desert, east of the Dead Sea). John, it seems clear, must be out of the way before Jesus begins his ministry. Lk prefers to clear preceding actors off the stage to concentrate on subsequent ones. We have already seen him do this repeatedly in the seven scenes of his infancy narrative. Note how John fails to appear even in the following baptismal scene of #6. Lk does *not* present the Baptist as another Elijah—as do Mk 1:6 and Mt 3:4—except briefly in 1:17.

For Lk, it is Jesus who is the new Elijah (cf. 7:11-16 = G.P. #80 which is a parallel to the Elijah story of 1 Kg 17).

In #10 Lk speaks of the rejection at Nazareth, a combination surely of a group of incidents whose lack of chronological accuracy is revealed in 4:23 since Lk has not yet spoken of Jesus' activity in Capernaum. Lk's purpose here is to present a preview of Christ's whole ministry: Old Testament fulfillment (vv. 18-21); initial acceptance (22); rejection (24-28); death (29). Lk has also managed to stress universal salvation (and the story of the Church in Acts) by emphasizing (vv. 25-27) the salvation extended by Elijah and Elisha to the Gentiles. It is theologically exciting to note what saved these Gentiles: *bread* in the case of the widow of Zarephath (1 Kg 17:8-16) and *water* in the instance of Naaman (2 Kg 5:14). Surely Lk is telling all attentive readers that salvation is extended to the Gentiles through bread (the Eucharist) and water (baptism).

Lk has also moved #11, the call of the first disciples, to a slightly later position, #17, even though this means that in Lk the healing of Simon's mother-in-law (#13) occurs with no previous introduction of Simon. For this same reason Lk must drop "Andrew with James and John" (Mk 1:29) from the story. He will also reverse Mk's order of G.P. #71-72 to place The Call of the Twelve (Lk 6:12-16) before Jesus Heals the Multitudes (Lk 6:17-19). By this reversal of sequence Lk can get Jesus off the hills (Lk 6:12) where he chose his disciples down to the plain (6:17) where he can meet the sick and disabled who become part of the audience for the sermon that follows. Apart from these few exceptions, Lk follows the Markan order.

In content, too, there are some Lukan peculiarities in this opening section on Jesus' ministry. Lk has surely prolonged the quotation from Is 40:3 found in Mk 1:3 and Mt 3:3 (G.P. #1) to include Is 40:4-5. By so doing he has incorporated into his Good News *the* good news: *"all flesh* shall see the salvation of God." This interest in universal salvation is a Lukan emphasis observable also in Lk 3:38 where Lk traces Jesus' origin back not merely to David and Abraham (Jewish forefathers), but to Adam and to God himself, thus including the points of origin of all peoples.

The temptation episode (#8) presents an obvious simplicity on the part of Mk's two verses (1:12-13) in comparison to both Mt and Lk. It would appear that the story used by the latter two has been built up to reflect (1) Jesus' superiority to Moses' Israel which succumbed to temptation in the desert and (2) the types of temptations to false messiahship which Jesus actually suffered during his own lifetime. It is illuminating to read in John's Gospel of similar temptations. In Jn 6:15 Jesus flees to the mountains, avoiding an attempt to make him king; in 6:26-34 he is asked to perform a bread miracle; in 7:1-4 he is tempted to be a spectacular wonder-worker. These temptations during Jesus' life parallel those in the desert temptation outlined by Lk and Mt.

The call of the first disciples (#11) has been expanded in Lk's #17 to concretize, by means of the miraculous catch, the disciples' mission as fishers of the followers of Jesus (cf. exemplar on p. 27).

One small but significant Lukan specialty occurs in #70 where Lk 6:10 follows Mk's phrase, "And he looked around" (Mk 3:5), but omits Mk's subsequent reference to anger. That is not the kind of emotion that Lk is interested in.

(ii) Sermon on the Plain (6:20-49 = G.P. #73-78)

Lk's Sermon on the Plain centers on the theme of charity which manifests itself in action. Considerably shorter than Mt's Sermon on the Mount which runs through three chapters, Lk's version is short, consolidated and full of impact. It speaks in the second person. "Blessed are *you* poor . . . *you* that hunger," etc., in contrast to Mt's use of the generic third person, "Blessed are the poor in spirit . . . those who mourn . . . those who hunger . . . ." (G.P. #73).

In verses 20-26 Lk gives us a carefully balanced presentation of blessings and woes.

20—blessed are you poor	24—woe to you rich
21—blessed you who hunger	25—woe to you full
21b—blessed you that weep	25—woe to you who laugh
22—blessed when men hate you	26—woe when men speak well of you
23—for so their fathers did to the prophets	26b—for so their fathers did to the false prophets

Verses 27-36 focus on love of one's enemies. In v. 27 Lk joins together *hearing and doing,* a Christian formula for living to which we will see him return often. The Lukan material here has close parallels in Mt (underline for verification), but the two are not literally identical, nor do their elements follow the same sequence. Lk's material in these verses is paralleled in Mt 5:44, 39-42; 7:12; 5:46-47, 45, 48—all in Mt's Sermon on the Mount. It is difficult to imagine that either Lk or Mt has a copy of the other's Gospel which he is rearranging in this fashion. It is much more probable that both are working with similar sources.

6:36 reads "Be *merciful,* as your Father is *merciful,"* rather than Mt 5:48, ". . . be *perfect* as your heavenly Father is *perfect."* Mt's context is love, and for him, love means being perfect like the Father. Lk says much the same, except that he epitomizes love and perfection in mercy. Verses 37-42 ask that we judge not. Lk is here paralleled by Mt 7:1-2; 15:14; 10:24-25; 7:3-5, with only the passages from Mt 7 being found in the Sermon on the Mount. It is only in the final verses (Lk 6:41-42 = Mt 7:3-5) that we get almost identical wording. These same verses provide another excellent example of Q.

6:43-49 (#77-78) insists on a Christian matching theory with practice, hearing with doing. And note how Lk's v. 45 twice mentions the inner heart, the true internal disposition which produces good or evil.

This Lukan section again has parallels in Mt 7:16-21, 24-27 and 12:33-35. Yet their common material must have been somewhat changed before reaching them, or through the changes rendered necessary as the evangelists preached it to differing congregations, perhaps in different countries. In #78 Lk's version envisions a man who must dig deeply to find rock. In Mt the rocky ground seems to be there for the asking. Mt's foolish man builds on sand. Lk's parallel speaks not of sand but simply a house with no foundation.

"After he had ended all his sayings . . ." (Lk 7:1) may sound like Mt's famous book-ends, but not a single word is the same in the Greek texts.

(iii) 7:1-8:3. Lk's Sermon on the Plain has now ended but, as is evident in the G.P. Index, Lk includes #79-84 before joining up again with Mk's parable of the sower in #90. Perhaps what Lk is doing at this point is offering a series of people who illustrate the words of the sermon, "Everyone who comes to me and hears my words and does them, I will show you what he is like . . ." (6:47). In any case, Lk now presents:

—a pagan centurion in 7:1-10 (#79). This long-distance cure is a foreshadowing of the future mission to the Gentiles and, as we have seen above on p. 73, an intended parallel to the story of the centurion Cornelius in Acts 10. It is with the thought of Cornelius in mind, and the realization of the critical position he occupied in the turning of salvation to the Gentiles, that Jesus' extravagant praise takes on its full impact: "I tell you, not even in Israel have I found such faith" (Lk 7:9).

—a widowed mother at Nain "who weeps now" (cf. Lk 6:20) over her dead son (7:11-17). The spontaneity of Jesus' charity appears in 7:13, "he had compassion on her. This incident is found only in Lk who uses it to parallel the Elijah and Elisha miracles of 1 Kg 7:17ff. and 2 Kg 4:18ff. Elijah resuscitates the dead son of a widow. The words of Lk 7:15, "And he gave him to his mother," are identical in Greek to those of 1 Kg 17:23. For Lk, Jesus is the new Elijah. "A great prophet has arisen among us" (7:16). We have already seen Lk's interest in Elijah's widow and her son in 4:26.

This may have reminded Lk of the response to the Baptist, ". . . the dead are raised up" (7:22) so that he inserts here this Baptist material. Mt used this same material elsewhere, in his specially constructed ch. 11, to present reactions to Jesus, the hidden Wisdom of God, in preparation for the parable discourse.

Lk then continues to present:
—a sinful but loving woman (7:36-50). Lk's care for both sinners and women is especially evident here. There is a magnificent tying together of sin, faith, and love. ". . . her *sins* which are many are forgiven, for she *loved* much . . . . Your *faith* has saved you; go in peace." One is reminded of Paul's theology in Gal 5:5-6 in which righteousness depends on "faith working through love." This story of the anointing by the sinful woman has close resemblance—original identity?—to the anointing story presented by Mk and Mt at the beginning of the passion account (#232). For that reason Lk will omit it at that juncture.

—ministering women who accompanied Jesus. Lk's mention here of "the twelve (who) were with him" reminds him of the women also who gave Jesus their support: "Mary called Magdalene . . . and Joanna, the wife of Chuza, Herod's steward, and Susanna, and many others who provided for them out of their means." Joanna and her husband could have been a special source for Lk's frequent mention of the family of Herod (3:1, 19; 8:3; 9:7, 9; 13:31; 23:7-15; Acts 4:27; 12:1-23; 13:1; 25:13-26:32).

(iv) 8:4-9:50
In this section Lk returns to the basic Markan sequence (cf. G.P. #90) which he will follow with the notable exception of his Great Omission of #113-121.

Lk 8:4-21 ties two sections together, the Parable of the Sower and Jesus' True Relatives (cf. #90, 91, 93, 94, 104). Lk takes from the three Markan parables only that of the sower. He abbreviates it and in his presentation (vv. 11-15 = #93) accentuates "hear . . . believe and be saved . . . hearing the word, hold it fast in an honest and good heart, and bring forth fruit with patience." This combination of salvation through belief in the word, holding it fast in patience and producing fruit is strongly Pauline. It appears here in Lk in strong contrast to the presentation in both Mk and Mt. Lk has tied to this parable #104 (Lk 8:19-21, Jesus' True Relatives) which is found at this point only in Lk. (Note its position at #84 in Mk and Mt.) In so doing, Lk presents Jesus' mother and family as being among those "who hear the word of God and do it" (v. 21). This is consistent with Lk's presentation of Mary in the infancy narrative as obedient to God's word (1:38) and as meditative of the divine message (2:19, 51). It also agrees with Lk's picture of Mary and the brethren in Acts 1:14.

Lk's presentation of #105-106, the Stilling of the Storm and the Gerasene Demoniac, are very similar to Mk's. Worthy of note, however, is the difference found at the end of #106 where Mk's text in 5:19-20, ". . .tell them how much the *Lord* (Kurios) has done for you . . . how much *Jesus* has done" has been changed in Lk 8:39 to "how much *God* (Theos) has done for you . . . how much *Jesus* had done." Mk equates Lord and Jesus: Lk equates Jesus and God.

The story of Jairus' daughter has subtle Lukan touches when compared to Mk. Mk's verse 26, which is so rough on physicians, disappears in Lk. Readers sympathetic to the idea that our author is himself Luke the physician of Col 4:14 can find support in this unwillingness to treat doctors with Markan disrespect. The brusque, rather disrespectful question of the disciples in Mk's v. 31 also disappears in Lk. And, finally, Mk's Aramaic *"Talitha cumi"* (v. 41) is also omitted by Lk whose audience, we can begin to suspect, would have been incapable of understanding the expression.

The Sending Out of the Twelve in #109 shows little difference from Mk, but #110-111 give a significant view into Lk's personality. He seems content enough in #110 to mention, with Mk, Herod's perplexity regarding Jesus' identity, but in #111 the Lukan column shows up missing. Not a word is given of the whole bloody and shameful story of John's severed head and the maiden's shimmering hips. That is simply not Lk's cup of tea.

#112 is Lk's version of the Feeding of the 5,000. It is a stripped down edition of Mk's text, giving the impression—which will be justified in subsequent events—that Lk is trying to save space. This probably accounts for Lk's mention of Bethsaida in v. 10 (to be found in Mk 6:45 which Lk will skip over). This makes Lk's text ambiguous. Does the feeding take place in Bethsaida (v. 10) or in a lonely place (v. 12)? The verbs of v. 16—taking, blessed, broke, gave—have the character of Eucharistic regulations for the celebrant and have probably been influenced by the Church's Eucharistic practice. The function of intermediaries performed by the disciples (v. 16) may intend to insinuate a continuing Eucharistic ministry to Lk's Church, for there were baskets "left over" for subsequent feedings.

What happens next in Lk is what does not happen, Lk's Great Omission, evident in G.P. Index #113-121 as the Lukan column goes completely blank. The most likely explanation for this is that Lk is beginning to feel pinched for space. The length of a Greek literary scroll had a maximum of thirty to thirty-five feet, and Lk still had much material—including his own Special Section from 9:51-18:14—to include. So he omits Mk 6:45-8:26 with the justification that it contains incidents similar to others in the

Gospel (e.g., #113 is similar to #105, #114 to #71, #118 to #112, #119 to #149), incidents overly Jewish (#115, 116, 120), or somewhat offensive (#116, 117, 121).

From 9:18-50 (#122-130) Lk returns to the Markan sequence, except that he eliminates #125, The Coming of Elijah, since, apart from 1:17, the Baptist is not presented as Elijah by Lk. A few special Lukan touches are evident, however.

—not suprisingly, Lk omits the rebukes by and of Peter in #122 (Mk 8:32-33).

—He adds "daily" in #123 (Lk 9:23) to apply a figurative crossbearing to the Christian's daily life.

—He also adds the very illuminating phrase in #124 (Lk 9:31): ". . . who appeared in glory and spoke of his *departure* which he was to accomplish at Jerusalem." I say illuminating, when we realize that the Greek original to our "departure" translation is *exodos*. Lk wishes us to understand that Jesus' death in Jerusalem will be his exodus, his salvation event for the world.

—In #126, Lk terminates the cure of the epileptic boy with the surprising "And all were astonished at the majesty of God." In Jesus' miracles is God's majesty manifested.

It has been suggested that Lk uses much of this material to answer the question of Herod found only in Lk 9:9 (#110): "John I beheaded; but who is this about whom I hear such things?" Lk's answer, in this case, would be:

9:20, "The Christ of God";
9:35, "This is my Son, my chosen";
9:43, ". . . the majesty of God."

c) LUKE'S SPECIAL SECTION (9:51-18:14)

This section is the outstanding characteristic of Lk's Gospel structure. The G.P. Index from #137-186 gives us only Lk in the first three columns. Only he follows this sequence. Between Mk's last unit at #132 and his following one in #187, Lk has inserted a large block of material, fifty sections, adding up to nearly fifty percent of his whole Gospel. This material is composed mainly of L and Q as you can see clearly for yourself by skimming rapidly through these paragraphs in the body of the G.P. (*not* the Index) starting with #137. Presenting themselves will be page after page of material uniquely Lukan (L) or which he shares with Mt (Q). Mk appears to have had little or no effect on this section, and this has led some scholars to speculate that we have here a Proto-Luke (First-Luke), something which Lk had put together before obtaining Mk and which he simply inserted into Mk at this point which he considered suitable.

For Lk there will be no return to Galilee after 9:51, "When the days draw near for him to be received up, *he set his face to go to Jerusalem.*" From this point on, till his arrival in Lk 19:45, Jesus will be on his way. Mk's *Way to the Cross,* found also in Mt, becomes in Lk a veritable pilgrimage of the victim to that sacrifice which will constitute Christian exodus. Lk has underlined with striking emphasis this journey from Galilee to Jerusalem, both by the length of the chapters it occupies and by this frequent references to it in 9:51, 53; 13:22, 33; 17:11; 19:11, 28, 41.

One Lukan peculiarity at the very beginning of the journey is his phrase in 9:51, ". . . for him to be *received up* . . . ." The Greek for this is *analēmpseōs,* the same word root as that used to describe the *taking up* of Elijah by the whirlwind in 2 Kg 2:9, 11. Lk will use this root again in Acts 1:2, 11 to recount Jesus' Ascension. Little wonder, then, that Lk, using so many Elijah references to Jesus, shies clear of identifying the Baptist with Elijah as do both Mk and Mt.

Lk shortens Jesus' ministry in Galilee to expand the travel section, using within it material which Mt (and, minimally, Mk) place within the Galilean ministry. Since so much of the material here is L, we should be able to gain insight into Lk by studying the type of passages he has been interested in enough to collect and organize for himself. These are:

#137 - the Samaritan Villagers
#144 - The Good Samaritan
#145 - Mary and Martha
#147 - The Friend at Midnight
#151 - The Blessedness of Jesus' Mother
#156 - Parable of the Rich Fool
#159 - The Servant's Wages
#162 - Repentance or Destruction
#163 - Healing of Woman with Spirit of Infirmity
#166 - Departure from Galilee
#172 - Lost Coin
#173 - Lost Son (Prodigal)
#175 - Hypocrisy of Pharisees
#177 - The Rich Man and Lazarus
#181 - Servant's Wages
#182 - Healing of the Ten Lepers—Samaritan
#185 - Parable of Unjust Judge

(i) There is a certain emphasis here on Samaritans, historically *the* enemy of the Jewish people, but, during Lk's lifetime, an object of Christian mission (Acts 1:8; 8:5-25; 9:31;15:3). In 9:52 and 17:11 Jesus journeys in the vicinity of Samaria; in 10:25-37 the Good Samaritan is the example of love of neighbor; in 17:11-19 the only cured leper to show gratitude is a Samaritan. Lk's Gospel picture of Jesus's ministry is already preparing its reader for Acts' description of the Church.

(ii) There is also an insistence on women: on Mary and Martha in #145; on Jesus' mother in #151; on the crippled woman of #163, for she, too, was "a daughter of Abraham."

(iii) Two of the most exciting things which Lk does in this section are his contructions of the complexes of #143-145 and #172-173.

—#143-145 = The Lawyer's Question, Good Samaritan, Mary and Martha (Lk 10:25-42)

It would be worthwhile to underline #143 to note the subtle but important changes being made in Mk by both Mt and Lk. Mt 22:39 modifies Mk by stating that the second command is *like* the first ("like it"), thus tying love of neighbor more intimately to love of God. But see what Lk has done! By changing the original question (v. 25) he has elicited from the lawyer a response (v. 27) in which there is only one rule, love God and neighbor. Not two commandments but just one: a single coin with two faces! And then

Lk continues—as befits a man for whom hearing and doing go together— ". . . *do* this and you will live."

With this, Lk, excellent preacher that he must have been, opens the discussion to the inevitable questions: "But how *do* I love neighbor? And how *do* I love God?" The two parables which follow provide the answers.

How to love neighbor? As did the Samaritan who, though the victim was his born enemy, met and satisfied his every need. Did the beaten man need instant care? He received it. Must he be rescued from the road? He was. Did he need someone to stay the night with him? The Samaritan was there. Who would pay his bill? His erstwhile enemy. And future expenses? This burden, too, was accepted. The Samaritan had responded with care to every exigency. And that is what it means to love neighbor.

How to love God? By sitting at the Lord's feet to listen and ponder his every word. By inserting this simple story Lk has accomplished a number of purposes. He has fully illustrated his one love commandment. He has also joined together two necessary Christian attitudes, the activism of the Samaritan and the meditative attention to the Lord's words of Mary. Finally, he has balanced off the sexes, using a man model first and then a woman. As we shall see later, this balance is a remarkable Lukan interest.

—#172-173: The Lost Sheep, Lost Coin, Lost Son (Lk 15:1-32)

This chapter has jokingly been termed Lk's "Lost and Found Department." *Lost* and *found* are the words—together with joy and rejoice—which tie the whole section together from their first usage in v. 4 till their forceful appearance in the climactic vv. 24 and 32, "he was lost and is found." The complex begins with a reference to the carping murmurers, "This man receives sinners and eats with them" (v. 2). Their place in the story will be taken by the elder son.

God is like a *man* who loses a sheep and rejoices immensely at its return. God is like a *woman* who loses a coin and rejoices immensely at its finding. Finally, God is the father who loses a son but rushes out to meet, welcome, and fete him at his return. The central point of this last story is simple enough to perceive—the presentation of God as a loving, forgiving and rejoicing Father. So, too, is the picture of the younger son as a child who breaks community with his Father, descends to the very bottom (swine) from which the only way to go is up, and who finds his way back again to the warmth of home.

But it is easy enough to overlook the powerful teaching concerning the elder son. His role is that of the Pharisees and scribes who say in v. 2, "This man receives sinners and eats with them." Even as the younger son broke community with the father, so does the elder son break with the younger whom he contemptuously refers to, not as his brother, but as "this son of *yours*" (v. 30). And just as the father ran to welcome the younger son, so, too, does he promote the restoration of unity between the two brothers: "for this *your brother* was dead and is alive; he was lost and is found" (v. 32). God is like a rejoicing man; God is like a rejoicing woman; God is like a father swift to be united to his son, swift to unite his sons as brothers. Chapters 10 and 15 do indeed show Luke the preacher at his best.

d) JUDEAN SECTION (18:15-23:56)

(i) Journey to Jerusalem (18:15-19:27)

At this point Mk and Mt begin the journey from Galilee to Judea and beyond the Jordan which Lk initiated chapters earlier. They present the divorce passage, a subject already treated by Lk in 16:16-18 = #176. But with #188 all three are together for the blessing of the children, the first time Lk is back with the other two since he began to insert his special section long ago in #137 = 9:51. Lk now follows Mk in

#189, The Rich Young Man;
#191, The Third Prediction of the Passion;
#193, The Healing of Bartimaeus.

Typically, he omits #192, Jesus and the Sons of Zebedee, which reflects poorly on these two disciples. Mt, in somewhat of a male chauvinistic role, shifts the request for glory from James and John to their mother. Perhaps he thought that a loving mother asking a favor for her sons was less blameful than the sons begging for themselves. For Lk, it is better to be silent about such mistakes.

Lk adds #194, the story of Zacchaeus, presumably because this story was situated at Jericho in Lk's sources and thus had to be united to the Bartimaeus incident which also occurred at Jericho. Zacchaeus, who believes that he is seeking Jesus (19:3) is, in fact, being sought by Jesus who "came to seek and to save the lost" (v. 10). And so today Jesus comes to stay at his house (v. 5), which means that today salvation visits the home of the tax collector (v. 9). The presence of Jesus *is* salvation. Lk, because he adds #194 here, must rearrange Mk's introduction to #193, which he does. If the Zacchaeus event occurred *in* Jericho, Lk cannot follow Mk's statement in #193 that Jesus was leaving Jericho. He also adds #195, the parable of the pounds. It may have been chosen for this position—Jesus going to his death in Jerusalem—to prepare the reader and the atmosphere for that event: "We do not want this man to reign over us" (19:14). An illusion to the destruction of Jerusalem is also present: "But as for these enemies of mine, who do not want me to reign over them, bring them here and slay them before me" (v. 27). There is another Lukan touch here, a desire to deemphasize in his readers an intense expectation of an immediate parousia: ". . . because they supposed that the kingdom of God was to appear immediately" (v. 11).

(ii) Days in Jerusalem (19:28-21:7)

Jesus is getting closer and closer to the city: ". . . he went on ahead, going up to Jerusalem" (19:28), finally arriving at the nearby villages of Bethpage and Bethany. In true Lukan style, "the disciples began to rejoice and praise God" (19:37), concluding with a refrain reminiscent of that of the angels at Jesus birth: "Peace in heaven and glory in the highest" (19:38). The emphasis on the destruction of Jerusalem (#197) is also Lukan, since he insists more in his eschatological sermon on the destruction of Jerusalem than on the end of the world (Lk 21:5-9).

In #198 Lk's touch is also apparent. According to both Mk and Mt, Jesus "entered Jerusalem." In Lk "he entered *the temple*" (19:45), the proper place for one who fulfills Mal 3:1, ". . . and the Lord whom you seek will suddenly come to his temple . . . ." From this point on in Lk, the temple seems to belong to Jesus as to its rightful owner. "He was teaching *daily* in the temple" (19:47, and cf. 21:37 and 22:53).

This stirs memories of Lk 2:49, "Did you not know that I must be in my Father's house?"

Lk omits #199 and #201, The Cursing of the Fig Tree, since he has already used a somewhat similar fig tree parable back in 13:6-9 (#162), and, perhaps, to avoid the harsh condemnation of the temple which the fruitless fig tree was intended to signify.

What follows in Lk 20:1-47 is a series of controversy stories which build up to the critical bitter confrontation between Jesus and his opponents. Lk's order here, #202-213, is that of Mk, to whose content Lk is also quite faithful. Lk eliminates #208, the Great Commandment, already used in 10:25-28 (#143). He has also produced a reordering of movement in 20:15, "they cast him out of the vineyard and killed him," which is opposite to that of Mk in 12:8. This rises from Lk's reflection that Jesus was first cast out of Jerusalem (the vineyard) before being killed.

Lk 21:5-7 (#212) is Lk's preparation for the Synoptic Apocalypse. Lk's verses focus on one simple point: when will *the temple* be destroyed? It is upon this one incident that Lk will concentrate. He thus avoids the more general question of Mk 13:4, "Tell us, when will this be, and what will be the sign when these things are all to be accomplished?" and the much more complicated query of Mt 24:3, "Tell us, when will this be, and what will be the sign of your coming and of the close of the age?" Lk, whose vision includes that of the Church marching across the plains of time (Acts), is considerably less interested in Jesus' second coming and the end of the world than the other two synoptists.

(iii) The Synoptic Apocalypse (21:8-36)

Reading Lk's material at this point (you can scan it in order easily in the G P by moving through #214-223, but skipping #217, 218, 222) makes it evident that he has lightened the heavy eschatological load of both Mk and Mt. Lk speaks primarily, and maybe exclusively, of the destruction of Jerusalem to which he gives unique attention in v. 20, "But when you see Jerusalem surrounded by armies . . .," and in v. 24, ". . . and Jerusalem will be trodden down by the Gentiles, until the times of the Gentiles are fulfilled." Here (21:8b) as elsewhere (19:11; 21:31, where he eliminates "at the very gates") he soft pedals any insistence on an imminent parousia. One might argue to indications of the end of the world and/or parousia in Lk 21:25-28, but world shaking language such as this is typical biblical sound effects to be used for any divine visitation.

(iv) The Passion Narrative (chs. 22-23)

The passion narratives, as we know, are marked by an amazing similarity in both sequence and content—and that, even in John. Because of this it is surprising to note the considerable independence which characterizes Lk's Gospel at this point. A list of the Lukanisms which dot these two chapters gives us a decent overall look at his theology and personal interests.

(1) Lk omits #232, the Bethany anointing, which appears in Lk in the form of a sinful woman narrative in #83 (Lk 7:36-50).

(2) He presents a cup-bread-cup sequence in the Last Supper in 22:17-20 (#236). The text as found in our G.P. omits verses 19b-20 which are placed in footnote "t" at the bottom of the page. But the overwhelming evidence of the best ancient manuscripts

demands that these verses be read as part of the original text. The mention of two cups poses no historical difficulty. The passover meal to which Lk refers (22:7-13) actually had four cups of wine. Lk would have been speaking of the second and third which were interrupted by the blessing of the unleavened bread and the passover meal itself.

(3) Lk is unique in presenting in this context the passage ". . . rather let the greatest among you become as the youngest and the leader as one who serves" (22:26). It occurs elsewhere in Mk and Mt. This passage, in a Last Supper context, cannot fail to remind us of John 13:1-16, where we are given, also at the Last Supper, the scene and theology of the washing of feet.

(4) Lk alone gives the prediction of both Peter's denial and later position of strength among the brethren (Lk 22:31-32). Some scholars have related this to the rock and key-keeper function of Peter in Mt 16:17-19.

(5) Only in Lk is mention made of the two swords (22:35-38 = #237d). This passage is the despair of commentators. Is the suggestion of v. 36, "And let him who has no sword sell his mantle and buy one," ironic? Does the statement in v. 38, "Lord, here are two swords" indicate to suspicious readers that the poverty of this insignificant Christian armory held no terrors for the non-Christian world?

(6) The mention in both Mk and Mt (#238) that the risen Jesus will go to Galilee disappears, as it must, in Lk whose Gospel will end purposely in Jerusalem. (Compare Lk 24:6 = #253 to the parallel differences in Mk 16:7 and Mt 28:7.)

(7) In #239 Lk is much gentler to the disciples than are Mk and Mt. According to Lk's version the disciples sleep but once, not three times as in Mk and Mt, and "for sorrow" (v. 45).

(8) Only in Lk does Jesus cure the severed ear in the garden (22:51).

(9) Alone among the Synoptics does the Lukan Jesus state, "But this is your *hour* and the *power of darkness*" (22:53), ideas which are strongly Johannine. Lk follows this by omitting Mk's sad commentary, "And they all forsook him and fled" (Mk 14:50).

(10) Lk has no *night* trial before the Council as in Mk and Mt (#241). Jesus is led to the Council only when day arrives (22:66).

(11) Another interest of Lk is to emphasize the innocence of Jesus (as he will that of Paul in Acts). Pilate repeatedly declares Jesus guiltless (23:4, 14, 20, 22). So does the Roman soldier in 23:47 . . . a decided change from the parallels in Mk and Mt at this point (#250). Rome judges Jesus innocent.

(12) Only Lk mentions an appearance before Herod (#245). Our discussion of Lk 8:1-3 already mentioned a possible special source that Lk has regarding Herod.

(13) The gentle Lk skips over the scourging (#246) as well as the crowning with thorns, the beating, spitting and mockery (#247).

(14) Lk alone introduces the "daughters of Jerusalem" in 23:26-32 (#248).

(15) Lukan, also, is Jesus' prayer for the forgiveness of his executioners in 23:34 (#249).

(16) The same is true for his promise to the good thief in 23:43 (#249).

(17) And in #250 Jesus' cry of desperation in both Mk and Mt disappears in Lk to be replaced by the peaceful, "Father, into thy hands I commit my spirit" (23:46).

These Lukan peculiarities in his passion account give us a veritable thumb-nail description of Lk's theology and personality. He is interested in Jesus as Last Supper model of humility, as was John (3), with whom he shares other concepts as well (9). He visualizes a Church-strengthening role for Peter (4). He is very interested in Jerusalem as the necessary culmination of Jesus' ministry (6). He has special knowledge of some of the details of the passion (10, 12). He evinces an interest in the women who appear in the passion story (14). He is intent on underlining Jesus' innocence, declared repeatedly by Roman characters (11). He is, above all, a man of great gentleness and mercy (7, 8, 13, 15, 16, 17).

(e) APPEARANCES OF THE RISEN LORD (ch. 24)

The Lukan appearance stories—apart from that of the empty tomb (#253) which he shares, in general, with Mk and Mt—are particularly his own and indicate his own theological interests. As we have noted, they are all related to Jerusalem, for "the word of the Lord (the good news of the Risen Jesus) shall go forth . . . from Jerusalem" (cf. Is 2:3).

The Emmaus appearance of 24:13-35 is heavy with theological overtones. Jesus "interpreted to them in all the scriptures the things concerning him" (v. 27). "When he was at table with them, he *took* the bread and *blessed* and *broke* it, and *gave* it to them. And their eyes were opened and they recognized him" (vv. 30-31). "As they were saying this, Jesus stood among them" (v. 36). Jesus can be found in the scriptures, is recognized in the breaking of the bread, stands in their assembly. Lk is teaching his community and the Christian communities of all times that the Risen Lord—as then, so now—is to be sought and found in the Book, in the Bread, in the Brethren.

Lk 24:36-43 is his insistence, especially necessary for Greek readers, that the Risen Lord was still to be identified with the human Jesus of Nazareth. Paul had a similar difficulty with the Greeks at Corinth (1 Cor 15:35ff.), as did John in 20:19-29.

Verses 44-49 tie Jesus once more to the Old Testament scriptures—in particular to that of the Suffering Servant—which these early Christians had no intention of losing or ignoring. Lk also gives a strong parallel to Mt's Great Commission as he mentions that "*forgiveness of sins* should be *preached* in his *name to all nations,*" that "you are *witnesses* of these things" and that he will "send the *promise* of (the) Father upon" them (vv. 47-49).

The Ascension finishes off the Gospel and unites it to the opening verses of Lk's companion volume, the Acts of the Apostles. Thus:

Lk 24:47-48 = Acts 1:8b;
Lk 24:49 = Acts 1:4;
Lk 24:51-52 = Acts 1:9, 12.

For Luke, the Good News is to go forth to all nations, beginning from Jerusalem (Lk 24:47; Is 2:1-3; Mic 4:1-3). Jesus' exodus, his sacrifice for all, and his resurrection occur at Jerusalem, and this has been the pronounced goal of his entire Gospel. This good news is now to be carried to the ends of the earth (Lk 24:47; Acts 1:8). But this is the story of Lk's other volume. For now the story concludes in Jerusalem and in its temple!

"And they returned to Jerusalem with great joy, and spent all their time in the temple praising God" (24:53).

3. Author

Tradition, which can be traced back into the second century A.D., has always connected this Gospel to Luke, co-worker with Paul (Philem 24; 2 Tim 4:11) and himself a Gentile physician (Col 4:10-14). According to this opinion, Lk indicates his presence with Paul during part of the history of Acts by including himself quietly in the "we sections" of the narrative, the sections in which, suddenly and unexpectedly, the account changes from the third person to the first person plural. The first of these occurrences is in Acts 16:10-17. The others can be found in 20:5-15; 21:1-18; 27:1-28:16. Luke, in this case, would be referring to such personal experiences in his prologue (Lk 1:3) where he again speaks in the first person, and would be an eyewitness to many of the events in Paul's life. He would also have been in easy contact (at Philippi, Jerusalem, Caesarea, Rome) with participants in the growth of the early Church and in a position to verify at least the broad outline of the accounts he describes.

There are, on the other hand, perhaps an equal number of scholars who believe that the author of Luke-Acts could not have been a former companion of the apostle Paul. They find no mention of Paul's writings in Acts, and no trace of his unique theology in either work. Just the opposite. They believe that the author of Acts presents a Paul who differs radically from the apostle of Paul's letters. Lk, they say, has a poor understanding of Paul's theology of Law, and he presents Paul as a miracle worker and outstanding orator, both presentations contrary to the picture Paul draws of himself in the letters.

The discussion is still very much in progress. In the meanwhile, attribution of both the Gospel and Acts to Luke, Gentile companion to Paul and beloved physician, is still a well founded scholarly opinion. Certainly if this Gospel was not composed by a man named Luke, it is hard to imagine why such a name, rather than that of a better known New Testament character, became identified with the document.

That Luke was a Gentile is the more obvious meaning of Col 4:11-14 where Lk is placed apart from the "only men of the circumcision among my fellow workers." This raises a considerable problem for those, like myself, who believe that the Gentile Lk wrote Luke-Acts. How could a Gentile have such remarkable knowledge of the Old Testament as is evinced by the author of Lk-Acts? The difficulty becomes considerably less if one believes—again, as I do—that Lk was a Gentile "God-Fearer," one who like so many important characters in Acts stood on the periphery of Judaism (Cornelius of Acts 10:2; Lydia of Acts 16:14; devout Greeks of Acts 17:4; Titius Justus of Acts 18:7, and probably the Ethiopian eunuch of 8:27) or that he was actually a full-fledged Jewish convert.

4. Time and Place

Here again, as with Matthew, we are reduced to conjectures. Lk, like Mt, must have written some time after Mk so that a copy of that first Gospel could have reached him. If Mk, however, was written in Rome about 70, and if Lk was with Paul in Rome at the time of his death in the 60's, it is possible that Lk could have had a copy of Mk shortly after it was first published. But it is probably better to date Lk to about the same time as Mt—somewhere in the 80's. If—as was considered a possibility in the Introduction to Lk—Lk and Acts were composed together, with Lk employing Mk, Q and L as special sources for his Gospel, we would be envisioning a time consuming process. But the conclusion to all this speculation is simply that Lk must be dated later than Mk, and that any time about 80 A.D. makes sense.

As to the place of composition, we are left without any positive proof, though the oldest tradition would place its origin in southern Greece. Written in Greek—at times, excellent Greek—and addressing itself to the theme of Light to the Gentiles, it could have been written in any community with strong Gentile membership. Numerous places qualify; none of them persuades. For the student convinced that Lk brought Acts to an end because Paul was at that time still prisoner in Rome and that Lk was with him, there can be grounds to localize the composition of the Gospel, too, in Rome. But the theory in no way imposes itself. Acts finishes in Rome because the Word of the Lord has thus passed from Jerusalem to the Roman capital. Where the Gospel was written, therefore, is unknown.

5. Luke the Preacher

I have spoken elsewhere (pp. 82-83) of Lk's superb organization of the Lost and Found stories (Lk 15), as also that of eternal life as gained by love of God and neighbor (Lk 10). In each instance Lk has put together a complex of three stories, each suggesting in the strongest way possible a preaching unit. Both groups are found within Lk's Special Section (9:51-18:14).

Similar groups can be found in this same section. Take, for example, Lk 11:1-13 = G.P. #146-148. The theme is prayer. First we are told how to pray—the Lord's Prayer. Then follows (#147) an encouragement to pray with perseverance. Finally (#148) we are told that prayer is always answered: ". . . how much more will the heavenly Father give the Holy Spirit to those who ask him" (11:13)? It is easy to imagine Lk preaching this Jesus-material at length, material which he has necessarily reduced here to its essentials in written form. Another prayer complex can be found in Lk 18:1-17 (#185-188). The first passage (#185) insists on constant prayer, like that of the widow to the judge. #186 speaks of humble prayer, like that of the tax collector. #188 presents the example of little children. Lk's total sermon tells us to pray without ceasing, but with humility, like little children.

It is surely an aid in understanding the nature of our written Gospels to realize how much of their content was first preached by the evangelists and others. Often what we are reading is, indeed, the teaching of Jesus, but shaped and organized into sermons meant to express and promote the faith of the Christian community. This seems especially true in the case of Lk.

6. Two Special Lukan Interests

a) *Prayer.* We have just seen that Lk's interest in prayer led him to form two different complexes on prayer in his Special Section. In them he teaches

—how to pray (the Our Father of #146);

—perseverance in prayer (#147, 185);

—infallibility of prayer (#148);

—the humility that prayer demands (#186, 188).

But Luke has an even more unique teaching on prayer than all this. It is important to note that the Gospel so often ties prayer to subsequent activity, with the Spirit as intermediary. *Prayer, for Luke, results in action.*

In Lk 3:21-23 Jesus prays at his baptism, the Spirit is given, and Jesus starts his minsitry. This sequence of prayer, Spirit, action is typically Lukan.

In Lk 6:12-13 Jesus prays all night. Once day has come, he chooses from among his disciples those who will be his apostles.

In Lk 9:18-20 Jesus prays and the disciples, with Peter as spokesman, make their first profession of faith.

In Lk 9:28-31 Jesus prays. This is followed by a discussion of his departure, his *exodus,* and then Jesus sets his face to go up to death in Jerusalem (9:51).

In Lk 22:41-43 Jesus prays in the garden, receives the angelic presence, and rises to face death.

In Lk 23:46 even Jesus' death is accompanied by prayer, after which he passes over to the Father.

The Lukan pattern that emerges from this is one in which prayer is followed by action. Why this happens is insinuated in the first scene (Lk 3:21-23) in which prayer is followed by the Spirit who leads Jesus into his ministry. That Lk intends this intermediary role of the Spirit is clear from Lk 11:13 where the Spirit is the unfailing result of prayer: "If you then who are evil know how to give good gifts to your children, how much more will the heavenly Father give *the Holy Spirit* (Mt 7:11 has "give good things") to those who ask him?" Lk's theology of prayer, therefore, is that when a Christian prays,

the Spirit is given,

and things begin to happen.

The Christian who prays begins to move, urged on by the Spirit.

b) *Women in the Gospel of Luke*

Women occupy a remarkably central place in Lk. Even a casual reading produces an impressive list of references to women. Even more striking is the fact that Lk frequently offers "men-women" parallels. It happens so often that a man story is accompanied by—and often subservient to—a woman story. The following is a sketch of uniquely Lukan parallels indicating the evangelist's decided interest in women.

(i) Zechariah and his wife Elizabeth are "both righteous before God, walking in all the commandments and ordinances of the Lord blameless" (1:6).

(ii) The annuciation to Zechariah (1:11ff.) is surpassed by the annunciation to Mary (1:26ff.).

(iii) The gift of the Spirit is given first to Mary (1:35) and Elizabeth (1:41). Subsequently it is given to the Baptist through his mother (1:15, 41), to Zechariah

(1:67) and to Simeon (1:25-27).

(iv) Simeon and Anna are paralleled in 2:25-38.

(v) In 4:25-27 Elijah brings salvation to the widow of Zarephath. Elisha does the same to Naaman the leper.

(vi-vii) In 7:2-17 the cure of the centurion's dying son is followed by that of the widow's dead and only son. And in the same chapter, Jesus obviously prefers the penitential action of the sinful but loving woman to the pietistic carping of Simon the Pharisee (vv. 36-50).

(viii) In 8:1-3 the reference to "the twelve" is followed immediately by mention of Mary Magdalene, Joanna, Susanna and the many other women who supported Jesus in his ministry.

(ix) In ch. 10 the parable of the Good Samaritan is followed by that of Mary and Martha. The purpose is to exemplify the command to love God and neighbor. Love of neighbor is modelled for us by a man, the Good Samaritan: love of God is presented to us in the person of a woman, Mary, completely intent on the word of the Lord.

(x) In ch. 15 God rejoices at the return of a sinner like a man who finds a sheep, or like a woman who finds her coin.

(xi) 18:2-14 give us two of the characteristics of prayer. It should be persistent like that of the widow and humble like that of the tax collector.

(xii) In ch. 23 Lk's description of the way to Calvary parallels the help offered by Simon of Cyrene with the appearance of the "daughters of Jerusalem who bewailed and lamented him" (23:27). If the man Simon helps Jesus enroute to Calvary, there must also be women present to express their concern.

Luke the evangelist is clearly no male chauvinist. For him the beginning of the Christian era, the beginning of his version of the good news, begins with the gift of the Spirit to two women—to Mary and to Elizabeth. And from that point on, from the very beginning till the joyous announcement of the resurrection, women remain conspicuously present on the very center of his Gospel stage. At the climax to the Gospel story Lk's women are witnesses to Jesus' death (23:49), to his burial (23:55), to the empty tomb (24:2-3), and to the resurrection proclamation (24:5-7, 22-24). In Christian re-creation as in the story of ancient creation: "It is not good that the man should be alone" (Gen 2:18).